Social Entrepreneurship and Neoliberalism

Social Entrepreneurship and Neoliberalism

Making Money While Doing Good

Carolina Bandinelli

ROWMAN &
LITTLEFIELD
INTERNATIONAL
London • New York

Published by Rowman & Littlefield International Ltd.
6 Tinworth Street, London, SE11 5AL, United Kingdom
www.rowmaninternational.com

Rowman & Littlefield International Ltd. is an affiliate of Rowman & Littlefield

4501 Forbes Boulevard, Suite 200, Lanham, Maryland 20706, USA
With additional offices in Boulder, New York, Toronto (Canada) and Plymouth (UK)
www.rowman.com

British Library Cataloguing in Publication Data

A catalogue record for this book is available from the British Library

ISBN: HB 978-1-78661-107-9
PB 978-1-78661-351-6

Library of Congress Cataloging-in-Publication Data Is Available

ISBN 978-1-78661-107-9 (cloth)
ISBN 978-1-78661-351-6 (pbk)
ISBN 978-1-78661-108-6 (electronic)

Library of Congress Control Number: 2019949815

To Silvio Bandinelli and Susanna Falai

Contents

Acknowledgements

I thank Angela McRobbie and Adam Arvidsson for having given me intellectual guidance since the very early stages of this project. I am also incredibly grateful to Tom Shane, who has helped me in the difficult task of transforming a PhD thesis into a book.

Research is a collective enterprise, and I have been extremely lucky to be part of an inspiring and supportive research community: I thank Alberto Cossu, Alessandro Gandini, Alessandro Caliandro, Paolo Ruffino, Tiziano Bonini and Vincenzo Luise. Their friendship is a constant reminder that academia can be something more than competing, measuring, ranking.

I wrote this book while working as a lecturer at the Lincoln School of Film and Media. I wish to thank my colleagues at Lincoln, especially Rob Coley, who has been always respectful of my research and writing time.

Finally, I wish to thank all my friends and family, some of which don't know anything about what I am doing, and so save me from collapsing into my intellectual persona.

There is a special person in my life, my brother Arturo Bandinelli: thank you for existing (cit.).

I am writing from a place called home: my house with Alberto. He has liberated my desire to write. He has liberated my desire.

Introduction

One warm day in July, in a small and cosy café in Milan, I am waiting for Veronica, an independent fashion designer. She finally arrives. She wears a long grey linen dress, coral polish on her nails. She tells me she wants to make clothes following a different 'philosophy': she does not want to exploit cheap labour forces in developing countries. Neither does she want to save on the quality of the materials, nor to follow the aesthetic rules dictated by mainstream fashion. Rather, she wants to do 'things differently', producing garments that 'last over time'. Sipping her double espresso, she vaguely hints at the 'economic, moral and environmental' crisis and declares that 'things must change'. The details of the auspicious 'change' remain mostly obscure, but the desire to tackle some of the backlashes of neoliberal capitalism is expressed enthusiastically.

Joanna, a Danish woman who lives in London, reveals a similar attitude: she wants to create a fashion collection involving the community. 'People need to feel actively part of the brand', she explains 'after all, fashion is such an intimate thing . . . we need to change the mode of production and include ordinary people, as many people as possible!' Joanna lives in a newly re-decorated flat in Shoreditch, One of the most hipster boroughs of London. Next to her house, there's a Wholefood shop, where a loaf of bread costs about four pounds. On the other side, there's a brand new bar that serves 'organic cocktails' in antique tea pots and plays vinyl records. In her minimalist living room, there is a canvas she is about to complete: 'I need to express my creative potential', she says, probably to offer an explanation for the painting paraphernalia spread on the wooden floor. Pouring red wine into a big stem glass, Joanna tells me about her career projects: 'I had been working for the big names, you know? But what's the point in working for someone else?' Of course, the question is rhetorical. 'So I quit my job and decided to set up my enterprise. . . . I needed to do something I believe in, something to improve the world, at least a bit!', she utters persuasively.

Alfredo is about the same age as Veronica and Joanna; he is Italian and lives in North London. He loves nature, hiking and mountain biking. He is trying to change the world too. In Italy, he worked for a major bank, earned a very good salary and was living with his girlfriend of ten years. He was ready to settle down. But he ditched everything. He could not stand working for people who did not share his 'values'. He felt 'depressed'. 'I needed to change', he tells me over a pint of pale ale: 'I wanted to do something to change how things are, I wanted to have an impact!' Following this drive, Alfredo has moved to London and now is trying to set up his social enterprise. 'I am a privileged person, and it's just fair that I give society something back'.

Veronica, Joanna and Alfredo are running very different projects, their activities encompass very different fields, and they have very different objectives. But they share the same desire to 'change things'—even to 'change the world'—and the will to do it through entrepreneurship. They are social entrepreneurs, often branded 'changemakers': well-educated, middle-class women and men, graduated in a range of subjects that span from engineering to design, from media and communications to economics and finance. They are characterised by their ethical consumer habits, and the firm belief that enterprise is the best tool to tackle social issues.

The fact that young people cultivate the project or illusion of 'changing the world' is nothing new. Yet, until a couple of decades ago it is likely that those who wanted to do so would have signed up to a political party or joined a social movement. Now, many people choose another option: becoming entrepreneurs.

ETHICS IN TIME OF CAPITALIST REALISM

How can entrepreneurship be redefined as the royal road to express One's will to change society? How can people decide to actualise their desire to change how things are by means of a business? These are the questions that I asked myself when I started this research. The choice of studying this topic originated from an authentic difficulty in understanding and making sense of the very possibility of something like a 'social enterprise'. Indeed, to someone with my background in leftist critical theories, these two words can echo two very different, even opposite, spheres of thoughts and actions. The term 'enterprise' points at the maximisation of individual profit in the context of neoliberal highly competitive market; the term 'social' indicates values of solidarity and cooperation. I wondered: How is it that many people, especially young adults, could think of the first as instrumental in the achievement of the latter?

To tackle these questions, I conducted fieldwork over eighteen months, from June 2011 to December 2012, in London and Milan, with secondary data coming from informal interactions and interviews in Florence. This is neither a comparative study, nor does it address the specificities of urban and national contexts. My intention is rather to maintain the international scope of the social entrepreneurship scene, and to reflect the perception of the social entrepreneurs I met, who think of themselves as part of an international movement. While of course local differences do impact on the material conditions in which social entrepreneurs operate, my aim is to go beyond methodological nationalism (Beck and Sznaider, 2006), to analyse the cultural discourses social entrepreneurs produce across national borders.

During the fieldwork, I met dozens of individuals who express the urge and desire to build a more just and equal society, and who wanted to do that by being entrepreneurs. I asked them how and why they think this is possible; why they have chosen to become entrepreneurs to 'change the world'; how they think this change will eventually happen. Certainly, social entrepreneurs' discourses could be interpreted as ideological – a product of false consciousness that ultimately hides the real state of things. In this view, social entrepreneurs could be seen as eloquent expressions of a neoliberal world vision that wants the social sphere to be subjugated to the laws of the market. After all, the promotion of social enterprise by national governments can be interpreted as the attempt to privatise welfare provision and transfer the responsibility for social wellbeing from the state to the people. I believe this is partially true. However, the fact that a growing number of millennials show a renewed interest in the common good, often renouncing financial security to embark in a risky enterprise should not be entirely dismissed. In fact, I argue it is symptomatic of an ethical conflict that marks the consciousness of people in contemporary Western societies.

The social entrepreneurs I met are representative of the delusion and dilemmas of middle-upper-class kids, who find themselves trapped in capitalist realism, the 'sense that not only is capitalism the only viable political and economic system, but also that is now impossible even to *imagine* a coherent alternative to it' (Fisher, 2008: 2). The impossibility to 'imagine a coherent alternative' thought does not mean that they are happy with how things are. After all, capitalism has let them down: they were the teenagers who were told to 'follow their passions' to be 'happy' (i.e. also rich) and who now struggle to make a living despite their prestigious degrees. Although they have meticulously cultivated their inner talents, the job market seems to reject them, or to offer positions for which these talents have no outlet. Indeed, many social entrepreneurs aspirants who I met considered themselves practically 'unemployable'.

Most of them though did not want to be employed by corporations, for they fiercely oppose their social and environmental externalities. To work without a cause was typically felt as a source of deep frustration, if not of sheer depression. In this respect, social entrepreneurs are indicative of the prominence of ethical values over purely economic motivation. They are no more in a position to ignore the malaise of capitalism. They belong to a generation that grew up eating snacks and fast food, before finding out they were contributing to the death of planet earth (and their livers). They are those who grew up thinking chicken breast was nutritious, and now they are horrified by yet another documentary on the meat industry. They found themselves caught in a post-crisis society where the decline of democracy, the environmental apocalypse and the threats of war and terror weighed on their guilty and well-intentioned souls like the predictions of a contemporary Cassandra.

WHAT IS TO BE DONE?

How to live up to such ethical awareness, in times of capitalist realism? While they don't believe in the myth of endless growth, social entrepreneurs (like most of us) are marked by a profound dissatisfaction with party politics, and a lack of trust in mechanisms of representation and collective action. They carry the burden of the economic and political crisis of the contemporary Western world: they are the offspring of neoliberal capitalism, but at the same time they challenge some of its foundational pillars.

As we will find out through the pages of this book, social entrepreneurs are immersed in the discursive and material dispositives of power of neoliberalism: they are financially precarious, believe in the power of the self and think of work as a means of self-expression. At the same time, they are aware that the current regime is unsustainable: they are left with no job security, they don't know if they will ever afford to buy a house or provide for their children, they fear the ecological disaster, and they are sensitive towards patterns of capital exploitations.

Caught in this painful ambivalence, they embrace social entrepreneurship. This way, they resolve, at least at a symbolic level, the conflict between the will to be autonomous and recognised as a valuable individual, with the need to act consistently with One's ethical beliefs. But what happens when ethics and politics are actualised by means of entrepreneurship? And how does this reflect or contrast the current neoliberal paradigm? Investigating the world vision of social entrepreneurs, analysing their attempt to reintegrate ethics and economy, is a way to understand something important about the circumstances in which we all live.

WHAT ARE WE TALKING ABOUT WHEN WE TALK ABOUT SOCIAL ENTREPRENEURSHIP?

Social enterprise is gaining momentum. According to a recent survey in the UK, 'over One in four people starting their own business is motivated by a social purpose or cause' (Unltd, 2015). Social Enterprise UK estimates 70,000 social enterprises in the country, 'around half of which were founded in the last five years' (Social Enterprise UK, 2016). Since the New Labour era, UK governments have adopted a series of initiatives to support and promote social enterprises. This led to the multiplication of satellite structures that 'champion the sector and lobby for it' (Bridge et al., 2009: 219).

When I first started the fieldwork in 2012, only a few insiders would know what I was referring to with the term 'social enterprise', while most people simply ignored its existence. Nowadays, the term 'social enterprise' is a buzzword, and is increasingly popular in a range of fields: from arts to social services, from technological innovation to the green economy. This undetermined status is reflected in the varieties of activities that may fit under the umbrella term 'social enterprise'. These include practices of Corporate Social Responsibility (CSR); businesses that produce sustainable products or services, operating in the so-called green economy; private welfare providers; enterprises that experiment with open-source production and the sharing economy; and also cooperatives and cultural associations, for example, community cinemas, libraries, cafes, animal shelters and so on; firms in the field of behaviour changing design (sometimes referred to as 'design for change');[1] and alternative finance projects such as crowdfunding platforms (e.g. Kickstarter) or blockchain technologies. The phenomenology of social entrepreneurship has a similarly fluid and composite character, it appears as mostly evenementiel: comprising myriads of events, festivals, online platforms, seminars, workshops, think tanks, conferences, lectures, camps, booklets, research papers, how-to books, coworking spaces, business clinics, incubators and accelerators.

Despite its heterogeneous manifestations, there is a conceptual core that pertains to and traverses its diverse interpretations and definitions. This is the idea that entrepreneurial means can be successfully deployed to have a positive impact on society: to make it more just, sustainable and healthy. Consequently, the social entrepreneur emerges as the champion of the collective interest, the better-suited subject to build a better society. This is evident in the public as well as academic discourses on the matter. Alan Fayolle and Henry Matlay, editors of the *Handbook of Research on Social Entrepreneurship*, claim that 'the main vocation of social entrepreneurship . . . is to meet social and societal needs that have not yet been addressed by the state or the commercial sector' (Fayolle and Matlay, 2010: 1). The website of the Skoll Foundation – One of the largest organisations offering funding and support to social entrepreneurs – describes them as 'extraordinary leaders' whose 'organizations are creating innovative models to drive equilibrium change – the disruption of social, economic, and political forces that enable inequality, injustice, and other thorny social and environmental problems to persist' (Skoll, 2016).

This emphatic language is often shared by politicians and laypeople alike. Former US president Barack Obama, at the 2015 Global Entrepreneurship Event, remarked that social entrepreneurs can help by 'lifting people out of poverty, combating climate change, preventing the spread of disease' (Obama, 2015). And virtually every social entrepreneur I met during this research embraces the belief that it is possible to 'change the world' using entrepreneurial means. The underlying assumption is that the enterprise may provide the framework to pursue the maximisation of common happiness. It is a form of economic thought and action is so combined with ethical and social responsibility, and sponsored as the best solution to the most pressing issues of our world.

THE REVIVAL OF ETHICS?

Social entrepreneurship is not the only current phenomenon distinguished by the effort to integrate social and ethical conduct with the production of economic value, that is to say, the dimensions concerning an understanding of the common good that transcends individual interest and private profit.[2] The reintegration of a social dimension in the production process has been at the centre of various experiments, with equally various political connotations. William Davies notes that after a few decades in which the term 'social' suffered from a stigma that made it sound superfluous at best, today it seems to have experienced 'something of a revival' at least on a discursive level (Davies, 2015: 2). He goes on by enumerating the fields that have been rebranded by means of the prefix 'social': 'social marketing', 'social return on investment', 'social valuation', 'social analytics' 'social network' and, of course, 'social entrepreneurship' (Davies, 2015: 2). In a similar vein, Adam Arvidsson, in his book *The Ethical Economy*, systematises the various tendencies towards a mode of economic production that is oriented towards and motivated by ethical values (Arvidsson and Peitersen, 2013). Although he recognises the purely promotional nature of some of these initiatives (especially when taken by big corporations), he also signals an authentic growth of the demand for 'social consciousness' on the part of the public opinion (Arvidsson and Peitersen, 2013).

This is also reflected in the rise of ethical consumerism, proved by the increasing number of brands that position themselves as ethical, and by the rise of CSR investments on the part of big corporations (Egan-Wyer et al., 2014). Although it is far from granted that actors in the market can be in a position to really promote ethics over profit (Bertillsson, 2014), and although ethical consumers' behaviour can emerge as a form of 'delegation' and 'illusion' (Waltz et al., 2014), these phenomena still reveal a re-birth of ethics in contemporary societies.

Social entrepreneurship can be seen as a crucial case study for the understanding of a wider phenomenon that sees the attempt to integrate social and ethical dimensions within the sphere of economic thought and action. This book explores how the spheres of ethics and sociality are re-defined by their close intertwining with entrepreneurship; and if this very intertwining can translate into a new political paradigm.

THE AMBIVALENCE OF THE ENTERPRISE

The fact that the category of the enterprise may connect and combine diverse orders of values and logic is something that emerges from the classic literature on the matter. In a sense, the capacity of bringing together different domains is not an exclusive prerogative of social entrepreneurship, but it is constitutive of the enterprise. Since its earliest formulation by Jean Baptiste Say and Joseph Schumpeter, entrepreneurship has been characterised by its inherent ambiguous character. Schumpeter uses the category of entrepreneurship to account for the 'creative destruction' that produces change and innovation (Schumpeter, 1989). Frank Knight pinpoints that entrepreneurship exceeds the domain of pure economic calculation and belongs to that of inherent uncertainty (Knight, 2006). And David Stark, building on Schumpeter and Knight, argues that entrepreneurship exploits uncertainty to create opportunities, and recombines multiple evaluative principles (Stark, 2009).

What we can learn from these remarks is that the enterprise is a substantially ambiguous entity and operates, we may say, as a kind of Kantian schema to connect diverse orders of values and logics. Kant used the notion of schema to account for the ways in which our sense impressions can be related to, and translated into intellectual categories (Kant, 1781). A schema is a double-headed Janus that can connect separate orders of values and logic. Entrepreneurship has the function of a schema in connecting the economic with the personal. This ambiguity is a necessary condition to understand contemporary discourses on social entrepreneurship. It is because of this inherent ambiguity that entrepreneurship can be thought of as a means to act for a variety of objectives, with a variety of resources. However, this condition, while necessary, is not sufficient to account for contemporary discourses on social entrepreneurship.

The meaning in which the term 'social entrepreneurship' has been used in the last two decades indicates something beyond the fact that entrepreneurship unfolds within a social sphere, recombines social resources, involves creative human agency and has social externalities. It rather signifies that the enterprise, in so far as it is a 'social enterprise', has as its main purpose that of ameliorating society, making up for its inequalities. Contemporary discourses on social entrepreneurship, building on the ambivalent character of this category, produce and are produced by a cultural phenomenon that sees a growing number of people actualising and expressing their own values and virtues by means of a business. Indeed, while the fact that entrepreneurship works across a range of logics and orders of values is part of the established theoretical *corpus* on the topic, the idea that the enterprise is the best means to express individuals' ethical values and virtues is less obvious. The adjective 'social' here communicates the motivations of the entrepreneurs and the core business of the enterprise. Following from this, I use the term 'social entrepreneurship' to refer to a cultural redefinition of social responsibility and ethic, and to signal the attempt on the part of neoliberal entrepreneurialised subjects to take full responsibility for a social, ethical and political dimension.

SOCIAL ENTREPRENEURSHIP AND NEOLIBERALISM?

Within the literature on subjectivity and work in neoliberal societies, the ambiguity of the enterprise emerges as a dispositive of economic reductionism. The enterprise has been widely understood as the building block of neoliberal governmentality, precisely because it produces and is produced by competition, hence inequality, therefore eroding the possibilities of social cohesion and ethical conduct.[3] Therefore, the fact that ethical values can be expressed through an enterprise, and the collective interest can be pursued by individual entrepreneurs, comes out like a blunt oxymoron.

As William Davies put it: To argue in favour of competition and competitiveness is necessarily to argue in favour of inequality, given that competitive activity is defined partly by the fact that it pursues an unequal outcome (Davies, 2014: 36). And the enterprise is the basic unit of the dynamics of competition, for it articulates the character of a form of life that acts within a space of autonomy and uncertainty and whose actions are evaluated according to their success and efficacy, which, in turn, are measured in economic terms.

This implies the atomisation of the individual who, in so far as he or she perceives herself or himself to be an entrepreneur, will have 'only competitors' therefore equally unequal rivals (Donzelot, 2008: 30). Neoliberal governmentality is defined exactly by the process of de-solidarisation and de-ethicalisation of individuals and society, which is effected by remodelling people and services in the form of the enterprise. This implies a profound economic reductionism that de facto results in the subsumption of ethics and politics into the sphere of calculus and measure. Davies refers to this process as the neoliberal 'disenchantment of politics', that is, the 'deconstruction of the language of the "common good" or the "public"' (Davies, 2014: 3). He argues that:

> If liberalism treated the 'economic', the 'social' and the 'political' as separate spheres, with their own discrete modes of evaluation, neoliberalism evaluates all institutions and spheres of conduct according to a single economic concept of value.
>
> (Davies, 2014: 20)

In this scenario, the idea of acting for the collective good by means of the enterprise sounds, at the very least, weak. In principle, entrepreneurial ethos should lead the subject towards a kind of conduct that cannot consider other factors besides the maximisation of individual profit. Indeed, within an economic interpretation, private interest is the only criterion on which to assess the value of One's actions: the social, ethical and political dimensions transcend its limits and are therefore foreclosed.

Social entrepreneurs openly challenge these statements. The very fact of assuming entrepreneurial means are appropriate for the construction of a more equal and democratic, as well as more efficient, society entails a reworking of the neoliberal regime of truth according to which the market dynamic is substantially aimed at the accumulation of wealth. Indeed, as I will illustrate throughout this thesis, social entrepreneurship discourses and practices imply and indicate a decoupling between the market system (in particular, the entrepreneurial economy) and the ethics of profit. It looks as if the *homo economicus* entrepreneur of the self has become able to co-operate.

Of course, social entrepreneurs' claims could be seen as discursive and affective dispositives of neoliberal governmentality that hijacks ethical feelings towards economic actions, ultimately reducing the first to the latter. It is not my intention to argue against these hypotheses; indeed, they are quite convincing considering that social entrepreneurs, as a matter of fact, operate in neoliberal societies. Yet, I believe they still signal the attempt and desire to express and actualise ethical feelings and social responsibility. The 'common good' may be misunderstood by them (who is to judge?) but it is not altogether 'invisible'. And while they might not be able to reach social cohesion, they do regard it as a value. In other words, an affective attachment towards a form of responsibility towards the others is at stake, although it may be not fully consistent and formalised.

For this reason, I propose to take seriously the inner ambivalence of social entrepreneurship that, like a double-headed Janus, points to the subsumption of the social within the market logic, and to the decoupling of the market and the logic of profit. It enacts an 'assemblage' within the heterogeneous elements of competition, individualism and profit on the One hand, and solidarity, collectivity and social engagement on the other. Rather than resolving this ambivalence through a dialectical movement, this book represents the endeavour to delve into it.

To do so, I conduct an exploration of the main traits of social entrepreneurship discourses in so far as they reverse – at least on a rhetorical level – the relationship between ethical and economic thoughts and actions, deciphering the two as directly proportional. The questions from which such a reflection has originated are relatively simple, yet essential: How can something like a social enterprise be thinkable? How does One have to redefine entrepreneurial tools so as to think of them as adequate for a social ethical and political action? And what kind of sociality, ethics and politics are at stake?

WHO ARE THE SOCIAL ENTREPRENEURS?

The participants of this research are mostly young, well-educated, middle-class adults operating in urban contexts. They are an international crowd: most of them have moved to a big city – London or Milan – from smaller towns, or from another country, in the aim of getting a top-quality education, and building a successful career. Their lives in most cases involve a lot of travelling both for work and to catch up with friends, family and partners. The vast majority of them had to financially sustain themselves by means of part-time jobs in shops, restaurants or corporations, while using their free time to design their social enterprise. Alternatively, they could leverage their parents' resources, or on their personal savings, which enabled them to work on their projects underpaid or for free. As a matter of fact, it is hard to make a living as an entrepreneur, and for quite a few participants social entrepreneurship has remained a passion that could never translate into a wage-earning activity.

At the time of fieldwork, most participants were in the idea-generation phase of their projects and were not established yet. Their main concern was to build a network and gain a reputation in the field. Trying to become part of the network sociality (Wittel, 2001) involves the participation to a variety of events: workshops, conferences, networking events, round-tables, festivals, with the aim of establishing connections, meeting potential investors, partners and collaborators. In this respect, their professional biographies are typical of independent workers: their work schedule is unpredictable, their workplace is scattered in a myriad of different places; they work the long hours in coworking spaces, cafes and at home; the most common activity is to be in a 'meeting', which can happen in pubs; restaurant; on public spaces; or at home, on Skype or in person.

RESEARCHING A NETWORK SOCIALITY

During the fieldwork, I followed the participants in their fluid lives, doing ethnography at a variety of events: workshops, roundtables, seminars, conferences, lectures, networking sessions and so on, and tried to engage with them and understand how they thought of the social enterprise as a way to make money while doing good. While I did a few interviews, most of the data on which the following pages build on informal interactions: a chat on the tube, a conversation over dinner, a debate while having tea in a coworking space or drinking a glass of prosecco after a seminar.

At the beginning, such informal interactions proved hard to reach. Despite most of the events I attended were quite open and leisurely, involving organic cocktails, healthy food and indie music, everyone was quite busy, establishing useful contacts, catching up on the latest news and meeting potential partners. As an outsider, I found myself very ill-equipped to access the scene: I had no capital to offer, neither social nor financial. Trying to organise formal interviews presented the same difficulties: social entrepreneurs would often claim they had no time to dedicate to an interview for a doctoral dissertation, which is understandable: in a precarious reputation economy whom you speak and dedicate time to is crucial. After all, a PhD student is unlikely to provide useful contacts, smart business tips or investment opportunities.

However, the main obstacle to gain participants' attention was the difference in our mindset, values and conduct. Observing and over-hearing social entrepreneurs' conversations, I could pick a jargon that was still unknown to me. And when talking to someone, I would often find myself putting on a dull smile in the vain attempt to hide my ignorance about the facts and names my interlocutor was nonchalantly dropping. THIS made me reflect upon the importance of behaving, speaking, and thinking in a certain way to become a social entrepreneur. Or, to put it the other way round, it drew my attention to the fact that social entrepreneurs deploy a certain behaviour, speak a certain language and value certain things. To get access to the field, I needed to learn a specific conduct, to engage in a process of subjectivation as a social entrepreneur. This may be seen as just another way to formulate the main challenge of the ethnographer who, as Blumer put it, 'if he [*sic*] wants to understand the action of participants, has to come to see their objects as they see them' (Blumer, 1998: 50) and 'to place oneself in the position of the actors he wants to study . . . to take the role of others' (Blumer, 1998: 51).

UNDERSTANDING SOCIAL ENTREPRENEURS

It was thanks to the relationship and collaborations I established with One research participant, Alfredo – who I met at Impact Hub Westminster – that I gradually came to understand the world of social entrepreneurship from the inside. By trying to listen to what he was saying and having the opportunity to ask again if something seemed unclear or contradictory, I managed to decode social entrepreneurs' mode of thinking. This awareness was built over hours and hours of dialogue, where I put my own self and subjectivity to work, and in question. To illustrate this ethical labour, I share an excerpt from my notes:

> Today Alfredo told me of his new-born social enterprise, Social Enterprise Italy (SEI). When I asked him what the core business of SEI was, he immediately opened his laptop and showed me a slide reading: 'Our mission is to create a supportive and responsive environment to help the Italian social enterprise ecosystem to develop, grow, succeed'. I interrogated him about the actual meaning of these words, and he replied using the same language, still obscure to me: 'the idea is to create an organisation that supports the introduction of new models of organisation in the ecosystem of social innovation, working for different stakeholders . . . think of it as a platform'. I kept on asking for clarification as I could not figure out what sort of activities could qualify as supporting new models of organisation in the ecosystem. He tried to explain: 'Our role is to find changemakers in Italy, and then help them, offering them services, and then create the conditions for them to promote these services'. 'For example?' I asked, still quite confused. 'For example', he began, 'let's say we do a project in Bologna, we find the social entrepreneurs, we identify the ambassadors and then with them we come to the sale of services'. I struggled to understand what, in practice, Alfredo had in mind. 'The point is that SEI will offer a series of services in different areas: innovation, education, network creation. . . . I mean SEI will be a platform that could be used by a variety of stakeholders, and there will be many different services, but all functional to the maximisation of the social impact'. While listening to these words I could not help but wonder what sort of stakeholders? How do you think of a stakeholder? What sort of services? What does 'social impact' mean? How can you devise a service to maximise it?

Over the months, I often asked Alfredo these kinds of questions. He would reply to my doubts suggesting me to soften my critical attitude and adopt more 'positive' thinking. This tension between critical and positive thinking emerged quite a few times. Sometimes he would get upset by my queries, always directed towards the ethical, political and sociological aspects of his ideas, rather than the evaluation of and contribution to their entrepreneurial success. Once he told me: 'if you always criticise things, you will never be able to do anything!' I received similar critiques also from other participants. It was not rare to be asked something like: 'So, when will you start really doing something to make a change?'.

The contentions between Alfredo and I can be interpreted as conflicts between two different subjectivities, two different regimes of truth and power. And it was by comparing and contrasting his to mine that I started to understand social entrepreneurs' lifeworld. Because can there ever be an understanding of the other that is not also an understanding of oneself? Wolf, quoting Karin, aptly explains this reciprocal and reflexive process of analysis, as she puts it: 'Researchers . . . deal with two kinds of reflexivity – the self as both object and subject and the other as observed and observer' (Wolf, 1996: 35).

Certainly, incomprehensions were essential to identify the topics of my study: that is, the ways in which entrepreneurship can be redefined as a means for doing good, and what notion of change and political action is implied in this redefinition. And why so many people choose this route to live and work. To overcome such incomprehension, I had not only to better understand the participants' viewpoint but also to question my own position and biases

CHAPTERS OUTLINE

This book is structured as follows. Chapter I offers a brief overview of social entrepreneurship. It presents some of its main actors, discusses the prominent currents of thought in the new-born academic field of social entrepreneurship studies and analyses some examples taken from popular literature. The function of this chapter is to set the context for those that follow. Importantly, this research does not directly refer to, or draw on, existing studies on social entrepreneurship. Yet, this body of work is fundamental to understanding how social entrepreneurship constitutes itself as a field of thought and action, and what its main narratives are. The analysis of social entrepreneurship's academic as well as popular literature will lead to the identification of its conceptual core: the idea of doing good – even 'changing the world' – by means of a business.

Chapter II sets out the theoretical background. Starting from an understanding of social entrepreneurs as subjects who express ethical feelings and political values by means of work, I contextualise my enquiry in the field of cultural and critical studies of subjectivity and work. To begin with, I discuss the form of the enterprise within neoliberal governmentality, focusing on the figure of the entrepreneur of the self: an individual who conceives of herself or himself as an enterprise. After that, I delve into the individualised character of the entrepreneur of the self, in relation to the broader post-modern tendency towards individualisation. In particular, I highlight the anti-ethical and apolitical consequences of individualisation and entrepreneurialisation. Then, I move on to consider empirical studies of entepreneurialised workers, especially in the paradigmatic field of the culture industry, to indicate the tensions between passion, precarity and self-exploitation. Within this frame of reference, social entrepreneurs emerge as entrepreneurs of the self who try to re-embed a social and ethical dimension to their activities, and consider work the best way to express their values and virtues. In the last part of the chapter, I clarify my understanding of the terms 'sociality', 'ethics' and 'politics'. The chapter concludes with a discussion of the concepts of regime of truth and process of subjectivation and explains the extent to which they can be profitably applied to the study of social entrepreneurship.

Chapter III regards the sociality of social entrepreneurs at Impact Hub, a coworking space dedicated to social entrepreneurs. After having offered a brief overview of coworking spaces in general and Impact Hub in particular, I begin the analysis of the nature, significance and function of Hubbers' social interactions. Building on interview excerpts and fieldwork notes, I argue that social entrepreneurs engage in a compulsory and opportunistic sociality. To establish new 'friends' emerges as essential to further One's career: as a mandatory task. Such a task, to be successfully fulfilled, requires the development of a specific ethos, therefore a process of self-fashioning: an ethical process. This dynamic can be seen as a form of work organisation in which the production of the self is the condition of existence of a professional social status. In turn, this is vital to gain a valuable market position. But what kind of 'self' is produced? What are the main traits of the ethos that an individual has to embody if he or she wants to become a social entrepreneur?

Chapter IV tackles these questions. It is concerned with the analysis of the ethics of social entrepreneurship. I argue that the regime of truth of social entrepreneurship entails an ethical inward turn, where ethical needs are deciphered as part of the self to be actualised, and in this way reintegrated within an entrepreneurialised and conduct. This implies a private notion of 'change', rooted in the utopia of a world where everyone is a social entrepreneur. Moreover, this 'change' is thought to happen by means of the enterprise, a business organisation that needs to be profitable to survive in the market. This last assumption involves the redefinition of entrepreneurial means as ethically neutral and therefore appropriate to the achievement of a variety of objectives – from private wealth to the common good. This work of redefinition, which advocates for the distinction between 'good' and 'bad' profit, is One of the main tasks and aims of social entrepreneurs. However, it is problematic. To consider any tool as ethically neutral, therefore deprived of any peculiar agency, is *naïve*, to say the least. Tools have their agency and ethics in so far as they enable specific visions of the world, and actions in the world, while excluding others. The question of world vision and action enabled by the enterprise emerges as a crucial question for a critique of social entrepreneurship.

Chapter V analyses what types of actions and thoughts produce, and are produced, by entrepreneurial means. I maintain that social entrepreneurs display an evident ethical drive, and actualise it by means of business, motivated by the belief in their ability to 'change the world'. They are concerned with the creation of a future and they claim the responsibility and right to actualise it. In this respect, I consider social entrepreneurs political subjects. They are political subjects whose weapons are business plans, cash flows and branding strategies. What does this imply? What do these tools make possible and what do they conceal? I argue that social entrepreneurship produces and is produced by a form of post-political action and thought, with a prominent a-systemic and experiential character. Indeed, the enterprise can only enable local actions, confined within the sphere of individual influence and experience. While this can be an efficient way to tackle the effects of social issues, it will hardly deal with its deeper causes.

CONCLUSION

My intention is not to assess the authenticity of social entrepreneurs' discourses. Nor is it to emanate a final verdict on social entrepreneurship's value and success. Rather, I am interested in exploring the modes in which an entrepreneurialised and individualised subject can think of acting for the common good and taking responsibility for something that exceeds his or her personal interest. It is the very thinkability of this apparent oxymoron that I find relevant, for it touches upon a fundamental contradiction of contemporary societies. I contend that it may represent a form of social cohesion, ethical feeling and political action after capitalist realism. If sociality, ethics and politics are subsumed by the logic of capital, the enterprise may be One of the few forms that are left to express them. Social entrepreneurs may thus be seen as epitomising the struggle of the contemporary subject that is fully implicated in capitalism, yet suffering from its malaises.

NOTES

1. Behaviour changing design is a field that combines behavioural science with design thinking. Generally, it is defined as a technique to tackle social issues: for instance, a Design Council and Warwick Business School booklet states that 'the best way to solve social issues is to not only research how and why people make decisions, but use the design of products, services and places to help us all make better decisions' (The Behavioural Design Lab, 2013).

2. In the following chapters, in particular in chapter II, I will provide a more articulated definition of what is understood by the social and ethical dimension in the context of social entrepreneurship.

3. See, for instance, Lazzarato, 2009; McNay, 2009; DuGay, 1996; Donzelot, 2008; and Dilts, 2011.

Chapter I

The Rise of Social Entrepreneurship

Social entrepreneurship is a growing phenomenon, attracting the interest of a variety of actors: from politicians to successful business people, from academic institutions to third sector associations, from venture capitalists to charities. Social entrepreneurs have been promoted across a range of reputable outlets: for instance, *Forbes*, which every year nominates '30 social entrepreneurs under 30' as those who are 'Leveraging business smarts to save the world' (Forbes, 2019). National governments have supported social entrepreneurship, launching campaigns and designing ad hoc legal statuses. One example is the Big Society programme, ran by the British Conservative government from 2010 to 2015, which put social enterprises, charities and voluntary bodies at the centre of a public sector reformation. On 6th June 2013, at the Social Impact Investment Forum, UK Prime Minister David Cameron claimed that government needs to be more creative and innovative, declaring to social entrepreneurs that 'if you can solve the problem we'll give you money' (Cameron, 2013). Theresa May carried on the same line: despite the Brexit storm, on the 18th of July 2018, she hosted a round table for social enterprises CEOs (GOV.UK, 2018). Former US president Barack Obama has been no less enthusiastic, and has perhaps most succinctly captured the scale and grandiosity of social entrepreneurship's potential. During his speech at the 2015 Global Entrepreneurship Event, he proclaimed that 'helping social entrepreneurs mobilize and organize brings more people together to find solutions' for the 'challenges' that 'no country can meet by itself', such as 'lifting people out of poverty, combating climate change, preventing the spread of disease' (Obama, 2015).

Alongside state investment, enormous business funds are being devoted to the perceived promise of social enterprises. Jeff Skoll, the first president of eBay, founded the Skoll Foundation in 1999 to incubate, promote and support social innovators and entrepreneurs. Its website claims that it 'quickly became the world's largest foundation for social entrepreneurship, driving large-scale change by investing in, connecting, and celebrating social entrepreneurs and other innovators dedicated to solving the world's most pressing problems' (Skoll Foundation, 2016). At the time of writing, the Skoll Foundation has invested about $470 million worldwide (Skoll Foundation, 2019).

In 2003, Jeff Skoll, in partnership with the Said Business School (University of Oxford), launched One of the first academic centres dedicated to social entrepreneurship: The Skoll Centre for social entrepreneurship. This was an early instance of institutionalising social entrepreneurship in the academy. Since then, universities on both sides of the Atlantic have designed and delivered academic courses on the topic. Examples include Harvard, Yale, Duke and Columbia in the US; Goldsmiths University and University of East London in the UK; Bocconi and Cattolica University in Italy; the Copenhagen Business School in Denmark; the University of Liège in Belgium; and many others. In the last fifteen years, a number of scholars, mainly from business schools, have taken the first steps towards the establishment of social entrepreneurship as an academic discipline, with several newly launched academic journals being dedicated to the subject: for example, the *Journal of Social Entrepreneurship* in 2010 (Routledge Publishers), and the *International Journal of Social Entrepreneurship* in 2011 (Inderscience Publisher).

To further support the flourishing of social entrepreneurs, individuals have founded associations and international networks to support the implementation of social entrepreneurship practices. A significant example is Impact Hub, with which we will become intimately familiar in the following chapters. Impact Hub is an international network of more than 100 coworking spaces, comprising more than 16,000 members and explicitly targeted towards social entrepreneurs (Impact Hub, 2019). Ashoka is surely another important actor in the field: a global association of over 3500 fellows in ninety-two countries, supporting, promoting and building infrastructures for social enterprises. Its main slogan is 'everyone is a changemaker', a message designed to communicate the vision of a world 'a world where all citizens are powerful and contribute to change in positive ways' (Ashoka, 2019). Ashoka's founder, William Drayton, has made a huge contribution to the definition and diffusion of social entrepreneurship culture.

The list of associated businesses, charities, funding bodies and influential supporters goes on. Nesta (previously NESTA), founded by David Putnam in 1998 as the National Endowment for Science Technology and the Arts, and from 2012 an independent charity, brands itself as an 'innovation foundation' that brings 'bold ideas to life to change the world for good' (Nesta, 2019). Nesta champions social entrepreneurships through research projects, workshops and events. By contrast, Unltd (Unlimited), a UK lottery-funded charity, gives direct grants to emerging entrepreneurs. In 2017/2018, it supported 253 social entrepreneurs to develop their ideas and start-up (Unltd, 2019); since it was founded in 2002, it has given over 13,000 awards (Unltd, 2016b). The Italian landscape, although inferior in its scope, shows similar features: it is composed of a myriad of events, festivals, workshops, online platforms, associations and incubators. A notable example is Iris, the national network of research institutes on social entrepreneurship, whose aim is to gather, produce and communicate knowledge and experience on social entrepreneurship (Iris, 2016). The Italian ecosystem is further characterised by a growing number of coworking spaces and associations that work with local authorities to deliver social innovation at a local level. One example is AVANZI, founded in 1997 in Milan with the aim of offering research, consulting and incubation for sustainable projects of urban development (Avanzi, 2019).

The social entrepreneurship scene is dynamic, international and prodigiously well funded. Some of the most famous actors on the global stage have poured money, resources and hope into its promises. But at this point, we arrive at a fairly crucial question. What, exactly, is it? Can it be captured by a legal definition, or must we take recourse to a more conceptual framework? Is it yet to crystallise into a definable form, or is flexibility an inherent part of its nature? The remainder of this chapter is dedicated to building a faithful definition of social entrepreneurship.

WHAT IS SOCIAL ENTREPRENEURSHIP?

For a phenomenon that has received so much state and private sector support, these questions are remarkably difficult to answer. Alex Nicholls, lecturer and researcher at the Skoll Centre for Social Entrepreneurship (University of Oxford) and editor of the peer-reviewed *Journal of Social Entrepreneurship*, describes social entrepreneurship as in a 'pre-paradigmatic state of development as a legitimate field of "scientific" study' (Nicholls, 2010: 1). A pre-paradigmatic status is characterised by considerable suspicion over its academic legitimacy, lack of consensus over key research questions and methodologies, and lack of evidences in support of central hypothesis. Nicholls acknowledges that 'for some, social entrepreneurship is merely a fuzzy construct. . . . A projection of Baudrillan simulacra' (Nicholls, 2010: 1). Yet, this 'challenging context' (Nicholls, 2010: 2) makes social entrepreneurship a field demanding further explorations, and enhances its potential as an interdisciplinary research area (Mair, 2011; Seanor et al., 2011).

The difficulty in crystallising social entrepreneurship is reflected in the ongoing debate over its defining features. Definitions variously situate social entrepreneurship between the no-profit/for-profit spectrum (Dees, 1998;

Dees and Anderson, 2006), at the cross-roads of market, civic society and governments (Nyssens, 2006), in relation to the exceptional nature of social entrepreneurs, their skills and motivations (Leadbeater, 1997; Dees, 1998; Drayton, 2002), or even as a 'force creating society' (Steyaert and Hjort, 2007; Hjort, 2011, 2013). The divergence we can observe here is in part due to the diverse actors, and places, these definitions have emerged from. As Mair puts it: 'Social entrepreneurship means different things to different people. It also means different things to people in different places' (Mair, 2011: 16). From a purely legal perspective, social enterprises conform to different legal formats in different countries. As a result, national and international surveys and comparisons are mostly unreliable (Haugh, 2005).

In this regard, the 2011 GEM (Global Entrepreneurship Monitor) report on social entrepreneurship clarifies that:

> social activities manifest themselves in different ways – from a pure non-profit model to organizations that marry philanthropy with business models. Furthermore, social entrepreneurs themselves vary in their demographics (age, gender, education, current work status) and motivations.
>
> (GEM, 2011: 3)

Accordingly, GEM considers social enterprises those organisations that have an 'explicit or implicit' social mission, and includes not-for-profits that adopt 'innovative' processes, hybrid model enterprises (mix of grants, investments and revenue) and for-profit enterprises (GEM, 2011: 3). This results in a conceptualisation of social entrepreneurship decoupled from legal status or funding model. Instead, the definition hinges on the claim to have a 'social mission'. This definition could reasonably be criticised as vague, and characteristic of social entrepreneurship's 'pre-paradigmatic' (Nicholls, 2010) status. However, while the pre-paradigmatic status offered by Nicholls is helpful in expressing social entrepreneurship's unstable, manifold character, it presumes that eventually it will be formalised and find a secure 'paradigmatic' status.

Perhaps, though, social entrepreneurship will not crystallise into a coherent, stable paradigm. Its pre-paradigmatic status could be its imminent status. Put differently, perhaps social entrepreneurship will resist a fully fledged formalisation, taking various forms and traversing various fields. Such a quality may in fact be a defining feature of social entrepreneurship, meaning that GEM's definition, rather than being vague, expresses a fundamental component of social entrepreneurship: that it is flexible. Indeed, it is within this flexible field that social entrepreneurs are able to exert their agency, selecting or designing inventive solutions to tackle problems and adopting the business structure and revenue model they see fit. Recognising this constitutive flexibility can draw attention to several features of social entrepreneurship's 'social mission' claim: that it exists on a spectrum from implicit to explicit; that what constitutes a 'social mission' can be interpreted in a multitude of ways; and that the business model appropriate for achieving it can vary enormously according to the mission and the social entrepreneur's approach. Rather than considering these features as the failure of a vague definition, we can instead use it to observe that flexibility constitutes a core aspect of social entrepreneurship. As a signifier, it can be deployed in numerous directions, and this flexibility creates the space in which social entrepreneurs act.

MAKING MONEY DOING GOOD

If social entrepreneurship's flexibility creates a field of action, then the questions at stake in its definition begin to shift. Instead of asking what the social enterprise is (which leads us to legal statuses and economic models), we can instead ask what social entrepreneurship does: What is the objective for which the social enterprise is the instrument of action? What differentiates it from other kinds of social and economic activity?

The conceptual premise of social entrepreneurship is that entrepreneurial means can be used as instruments to effectively to tackle social problems. Indeed, most definitions of social entrepreneurship build exactly on the idea that market forces of competition and innovation, embodied by entrepreneurship, can be appropriate tools for achieving social justice. Fayolle and Matlay, editors of the *Handbook of Research on Social Entrepreneurship*, state that:

> Entrepreneurship can be an important way to restore a better balance between economic purposes and social well-being. Indeed, entrepreneurship can be a great source of economic value creation, but it can also be (or at least should be) a means to contribute to greater social justice.
>
> (Fayolle and Matlay, 2010: 1)

The characterisation of entrepreneurship as a technique to intervene in the social sphere is not something new. One of the first to promote this idea was managerial scholar Peter Drucker. It is worth quoting in its entirety a passage from his book *Innovation and Entrepreneurship* that, published in 1985, has become a classic of management scholarship:

> Innovation and entrepreneurship are thus needed in society as much as in the economy, in public-service institutions as much as in businesses. It is precisely because innovation and entrepreneurship are not 'root and branch' but 'One step at a time', a product here, a policy there, a public service yonder; because they are not planned but focused on this opportunity and that need; because they are

> tentative and will disappear if they do not produce the expected and needed results; because, in other words, they are pragmatic rather than dogmatic and modest rather than grandiose – that they promise to keep any society, economy, industry, public service, or business flexible and self-renewing. They achieve what Jefferson hoped to achieve through revolution in every generation, and they do so without bloodshed, civil war, or concentration camps, without economic catastrophe, but with purpose, with direction, and under control.
>
> (Drucker, 2006: 254)

Drucker defines innovation and entrepreneurship as tools for a reformation of society that is supposed to finally achieve those ideals of freedom and efficiency that revolutions and interventionist policies had failed to realise. Thus, entrepreneurship becomes an omni-comprehensive technique that can be taught and learned. This perspective on the enterprise as an accessible and democratic replacement of public policies is a marking trait of contemporary social entrepreneurship's discourse. Also, it evidences the 'tentacular' nature of the category of entrepreneurship, which allows to define it as a means for the management of virtually every aspect of life. The particular mode of thinking articulated here and elsewhere proposes economic (specifically entrepreneurial) tools as well placed, or even best placed, to intervene in the improvement of society. This is One of the core ideas of social entrepreneurship literature. Fayolle and Matlay write:

> Social entrepreneurship aims to better accommodate a social dimension within traditional economic behavior, to take into consideration social problems, countries' and communities' contexts and situations, and the plight of socially challenged or disadvantaged individuals. . . . It is in this way that entrepreneurs can contribute to the development of humanity and social progress – and social entrepreneurship appears to be a unique method that helps us rethink, reformulate and resolve human problems on the path to social progress.
>
> (Fayolle, Matlay, 2010: 3)

Fayolle and Matlay clarify that the objectives of social entrepreneurs should be 'social problems' and that the target of their small businesses should be 'socially challenged and disadvantaged individuals'. Entrepreneurship in this respect is conceptualised as an instrument, a 'method', that is well equipped to 'solve problems'. Entailed in the activity of social entrepreneurship is the presumption of having identified a social problem that has been accurately understood, the knowledge of what the solution to it is and the need for a financially self-sustaining enterprise to be part (or whole) of that solution.

Reflexive narratives of social entrepreneurship revolve around the same assumptions. An endless list of how-to books features titles that boldly reflect the very notion of changing the world by means of a money-making activity. A few examples are: *Your chance to change the world. The no-fibbing guide to social entrepreneurship* (Dearden-Philips, 2008); *the power of unreasonable people: how social entrepreneurs create markets that change the world* (Elkington, 2008); *the social entrepreneur revolution: doing good by making money, making money by doing good* (Clark, 2009). The latter – especially in its subtitle 'Doing good by making money, making money by doing good' – epitomises the promise and utopia of social entrepreneurship, the very core around which its mode of thinking revolves: a directly proportional relationship between profit and ethics, the money and the good.

The money emerges as both a means, a funding model for an organisation, and the ends, a nice life for the social entrepreneur. Michael Gordon, Professor at the University of Michigan and author of the book *Design Your Life Change the World: Your Path as a Social Entrepreneur*, articulates this very clearly when he claims: 'I hope to show my students each day, that you don't have to make a choice between making a living and making the world a better place. The same applies to organizations and business'. The targets of the book are 'the dozens, if not hundreds, of students . . . who want to address these issues and live lives of relative comfort' (Gordon, 2016).

Inherent to the activity of social entrepreneurship is the combination of private wealth – making money – and an ethical, social and political claim – doing good. The particular problem will differ according to the diagnosis and interests of the social entrepreneur. The means by which the enterprise derives its profit as part of a solutionary mechanism will differ too. This flexibility creates the space within which social entrepreneurs exert their agency and creativity. But the principle – making money doing good – is the conceptual core that differentiates it from other kinds of social and economic activity. It is the *sine qua non* of social entrepreneurship. Social entrepreneurship emerges as a flexible field of action for making money while doing good.

THE SOCIAL ENTREPRENEUR'S ACTIVITY BUSINESS, ART OR POLITICS?

How might we think of the action designed to make money doing good? Given that most social entrepreneurship scholars come from a business and management background and social entrepreneurship courses are mainly run in business schools, social entrepreneurship is usually approached as a business phenomenon. Some scholars have explored issues related to governance (Spear and Bidet, 2005; Spear, 2006) or entrepreneurial management, opportunities and risks (Pezzini and Zandonai, 2004; Jarvis and Tracey, 2007), while others have investigated suitable business models (Alter, 2006).

Helen Haugh identifies eight themes that characterise research on social entrepreneurship:

> defining the scope of social entrepreneurship; the environmental context; opportunity recognition and innovation; modes of organisation; resource acquisition; opportunity exploitation; performance measurement and training education and learning about social entrepreneurship.
>
> (Haugh, 2005: 1)

Efforts have been made efforts have been directed towards the identification and implementation of social enterprise models. As Hjort notes, 'This inevitably contributes to the re-description of the social as a form of the economic, whereby managerial tools become much more applicable and the managerial role correspondingly more central' (Hjort, 2007: 7). As a result, social entrepreneurship 'conventionally underplays the social side of entrepreneurship, making room primarily for the economic' (Hjort, 2013: 35). Clearly, as the 'social' in social entrepreneurship suggests, there is more to it than pure business. There is the good as well as the money.

Scholars such as Nicholls and Drayton have attempted to address this imbalance by deciphering the habitus, ethos and culture embedded in social entrepreneurship. Yet, they have done so in a mostly prescriptive way, leaving key aspects of the social unexplored. Important questions about the content of the much advertised 'change', about the meaning of the world 'social' when coupled with entrepreneurship, about the ambiguities and tensions that mark social entrepreneurship practices and discourses, have been dramatically overlooked.

Hjort's counter-manoeuvre is to conceptualise the social entrepreneur's activity as art. Building on his previous works (Hjort, 2003, 2005) and on the intellectual endeavour he has shared with Steyaert (Hjort and Steyaert, 2003; Steyaert and Hjort, 2003, 2006), Hjort proposes the notion of 'public entrepreneurship' as opposed to the prevalently managerial understanding of 'social entrepreneurship' (Hjort, 2013). Starting from a definition of entrepreneurship as a 'sociality-creating' process, he suggests thinking of it as enacting a 'desiring social-change' that cannot be reduced to managerial problem solving. Rather, it must be understood as related to art, for it creates new possibilities of life (Hjort, 2013). I quote at length a passage from his 2013 article 'Public Entrepreneurship: Desiring Social Change, Creating Sociality':

> In an attempt to place more weight on the social productivity of entrepreneurship, we inquire into the entrepreneurship-society relationship, affirming desire for social change (Steyaert and Hjort, 2006), and seek a new concept for thinking and expanding future possibilities of this life. We will use public entrepreneurship (PE) to make this differentiation. Our emphasis on entrepreneurship as a desire to create (novelty), which in turn is seen as what sets it apart from

> management's focus on utilizing resources efficiently, relates to art, as a practice sharing this effect upon the social. . . . Art and entrepreneurship create affect and intensity.
>
> (Hjort, 2013: 35)

Drawing on Foucault, Rancière and Deleuze, Hjort tries to redefine entrepreneurship as completely unrelated to individualism. He conceptualises it in a vitalistic and post-structuralist fashion, as a sort of 'energetic' that creates new assemblages, new forms of life. The Danish scholar advocates for a vision of public entrepreneurship rooted in the actions of citizens (as opposed to consumers) that create 'sociality' in a process of 'actualisation of virtualities'. (Hjort, 2013: 47–48)

Hjort's critique of social entrepreneurship scholarship is an important corrective, helping to reconfigure social entrepreneurship's activity outside of purely economic tenets which fail to capture it in full. Yet, the (openly acknowledged) performative character of his theoretical construction prevents the formation of concepts that can be used to undertake a rigorous critique of the ambiguities and tensions inherent to the relationship between the social and the entrepreneurial. Although it is true that social entrepreneurship's grand narratives overlook the social, Hjort's theory seems to deliberately leave aside the economic. By conceptualising entrepreneurship as a process, a power of creation, he makes it practically indistinguishable from any other human activity. Moreover, the focus on desire and affect in itself does not answer the question of their specific contents.

Albert Cho's appraisal of social entrepreneurship literature approaches from a different angle. Cho argues that the predominant discourses in the field are tautological and monological, for they leave the social undefined, as if there was an indisputable consensus about what it means to be social. An a-critical notion of the social, he argues, is responsible for the depoliticisation of social entrepreneurship because it sets the conditions for the question of the 'common good' to be evaded. In fact, this is an unavoidable question for a field that claims to deal with solutions for social problems and affirms to be better equipped to do that than national and international institutions (Thompson, 2002; Alvord et al., 2004; Fayolle and Matlay, 2010). As Cho correctly put it: Social entrepreneurship 'by its very nature is always already a political phenomenon' (Cho, 2006: 36). Indeed:

> When entrepreneurs organize their actions around values they have identified as 'social', they have already made demanding epistemological and political claims about their ability and entitlement to articulate what lies in the public interest.
>
> (Cho, 2006: 42)

Starting from this, he underlines the need for a 'dialogical' analysis of the values animating social entrepreneurs, One that can acknowledge the 'social' as a field of struggle. By identifying, prioritising, and articulating a problem, and framing it as both social and amenable to entrepreneurial intervention, the social entrepreneur takes political action even prior to the realisation of the enterprise. If and when the enterprise does materialise, its *raison d'etre* is then to effect political change; that is, to impose a vision of what the world should look like and how this change should be affected. This conception of the political echoes Foucault's idea of politics as 'what we are willing to accept in our world – to accept, to refuse, to change – both in ourselves and in our circumstances' (Foucault, 2007: 152). Marking the political dimension to the social entrepreneur's activity, we can refine our definition: social entrepreneurship is a flexible field of political action for making money while doing good.

TWO ETHOS: BUREAUCRATIC AND CHARISMATIC

What happens when social entrepreneurship's twin goals of making money and doing good come into conflict? This is, for some, social entrepreneurship's core paradox. The social entrepreneur is likely to continuously encounter decisions that pose a problem of needing to prioritise One over the other. And while sacrifices, trade-offs and compromises are typical in any enterprise, the social entrepreneur has two separable imperatives – financial and ethical – which may pull her in different directions at these decision points. What's more, insofar as social enterprises are more likely to receive public subsidies, questions arise as to how these funds are deployed – whether, for example, they are devoted primarily towards operational needs or towards managers' pay packages. After all, social entrepreneurship is promoted to those 'who want to address these issues and live lives of relative comfort' (Gordon, 2016).

Governance has therefore emerged as a central component of social enterprises as an attempt – and therein an admission for the need – to protect its social mission. Not only is this a defining feature of social entrepreneurship, it is from here, I argue, that some of the most salient conceptual themes of social entrepreneurship have emerged. The mechanisms of governance of social enterprises can be best synthesised as falling into two approaches. Drawing on Weber's concept of a bureaucratic and charismatic ethos, we can trace the development not only of two distinct mechanisms for governing social enterprises, but also the origins of the mythology that has since surrounded social entrepreneurship. In the charismatic ethos, we will especially see how the modern, mythical figure of the social entrepreneur has arisen.

The first ethos of governance functions through a legal guarantor of the social mission. This approach seeks to provide legal frameworks to externally safeguard the social enterprise's commitment to 'doing good'. Defourny and Nyssens expand upon this mode of governance:

> In Europe, specific governance structures of the social enterprise are put forward with a twofold objective. First, a democratic control and/or a participatory involvement of stakeholders reflect the quest for more economic democracy, in the tradition of cooperatives. They therefore add to constraints on the distribution of profits with a view to protecting and strengthening the primacy of the social mission, which is at the very heart of the organization. Secondly, those two combined guarantees (often involving a strict non- distribution constraint) often act as a 'signal' allowing public authorities to support social enterprises in various ways (legal frameworks, public subsidies, fiscal exemptions, etc.).
> (Defourny and Nyssens, 2010: 49)

The relevance assumed by elements such as 'governance' and 'public authorities' to secure the 'social' aspect of social entrepreneurship reflects the aim of achieving rationalisation and predictability. Social change is left neither to the uncertainty of entrepreneurship (Knight, 2006), nor to the creativity of individual entrepreneurs (e.g. Dees, 1998; Drayton, 2006). The attempt is rather to institutionalise patterns of social change, and make them part of a rational economic regime. This can be thought of as bureaucratic in a Weberian sense for it aims to build what the German sociologist defined as: 'a durable structure with a system of rational rules . . . designed to satisfy calculable continuing demands by means of a normal routine' (Weber, 2009: 245). This 'normal routine', assured by legal constraints, monitored and organised by public authorities, is meant to act as a guarantor of the non-capitalistic ethos and practices of social enterprises:

> Without these two guarantees, the risk would be greater that public subsidies just induce more profits to be distributed among owners or managers. In turn, such public support often allows social enterprises to avoid purely market-oriented strategies, which, in many cases, would lead them away from those who cannot afford market prices and nevertheless constitute the group that they target in accordance with their social mission. Public policies are also supposed to avoid that the neediest groups depend primarily on private philanthropy.
> (Defourny and Nyssens, 2010: 49)

This discourse builds on the antithesis between the profit-driven logic of the market and the ethics of a social mission. Because of this assumed heterogeneity between the two terms of the label 'social enterprise', a synthesis cannot be achieved without a further element operating as a regulator of the oxymoric relation. This element is governance, a legal structure that is meant to place the 'social' and the 'entrepreneurial' in the correct reciprocal position. Legal structure acts as the necessary condition for social entrepreneurship's assemblage of social mission and managerial mentality. In practice, it is expected to function as a 'constraint' to profit, and thus to 'strengthen' and 'protect' the 'primacy of the social mission'. Also, it is supposed to prevent social entrepreneurship from drifting towards 'purely market-oriented strategies'. Thus, governance functions as a protection for social commitment and the ethics of social enterprises, which would otherwise be jeopardised by market logic. It follows that social entrepreneurship is not conceived of as fully part of the market sphere.

There is an alternative approach to the social enterprise, which rather than intervening in the operations of the social enterprise focuses on the personality of the social entrepreneur. Scholars within this current generally advocate for social enterprises as fully equipped market actors, while recognising that a sheer market logic is unable to grasp the value produced by social enterprises (e.g. see Dees, 1998). Correspondingly, hopes are not invested in configuring a bureaucratic structure. In its place, this school of thought is concerned with describing and promoting a certain conduct and set of values. In other words, they seek to regulate not the enterprise, but the individual running it.

One of the first books to deal with the character and practices of social entrepreneurs is *The Rise of the Social Entrepreneurs* published in 1997, written by Charles Leadbeater, a well-known consultant who played a pivotal role as an advisor to Tony Blair during the New Labour era. In this work, Leadbeater defines social entrepreneurs as 'One of the most important sources of innovation'. He states that:

> Social entrepreneurs identify under-utilised resources – people, buildings, equipment – and find ways of putting them to use to satisfy unmet social needs. They innovate new welfare services and new ways of delivering existing services.
>
> (1997: 2)

> The focus here is on the qualities and talent of the individual that sets out to socially innovate. Following a similar line, Gregory Dees claims that: 'social entrepreneurship describes a set of behaviors that are exceptional', because they are a 'rare breed' (Dees, 2011: 4). Social entrepreneurs are described as charismatic 'natural leaders' that may operate in every field. Bill Drayton insists on this: The defining quality of leading social entrepreneurs is that they cannot come to rest until they have changed the pattern in their field all across society. Their life vision is this new pattern.
>
> (Drayton, 2006: 45)

The ideal social entrepreneur is supposed to be led by the need to positively impact on society. He or she is described as a visionary, almost a fool, someone who is able to follow an idea up to the point this idea becomes true. Drawing on the Weberian notion of charisma, we can notice that social entrepreneurs are constructed as charismatic 'natural leaders' who 'have been deemed possessors of particular physical and spiritual gifts' (Weber, 2009: 245). They are often placed within a typology of individuals that includes those who have 'practiced their arts and ruled by virtue of this gift (charisma) . . . by virtue of the divine mission embodied in that charisma' (Weber, 2009: 246). An excerpt from *How to Change the World: The Power of Unreasonable People*, the bestseller published in twenty countries, goes so far as to make explicit the social entrepreneurship discourse's theological tenor:

> Social entrepreneurs have existed throughout the ages. St. Francis of Assisi, founder of the Franciscan Order, would qualify as a social entrepreneur, having built multiple organizations that advanced pattern changes in his field.
>
> (Bornstein, 2007: 4)

The aim of these kinds of remarks is not to define and delimit a specific field of practices, but rather to build a discourse that focuses on some subjective traits that can pertain to different people engaged in different activities in different times and places. The analogy with religious movements is striking, because it excludes the economic and bureaucratic aspects from the picture, focusing more on the ethical, even spiritual ambition.

Perhaps it is not a mere coincidence that two of the most prominent ideologues and promoters of social entrepreneurship, such as Geoff Mulgan and Bill Drayton (CEOs of Nesta and Ashoka, respectively) had gone through a period of spiritual initiation before becoming advocates of social entrepreneurship. Mulgan trained as a Buddhist monk in Sri Lanka, while Drayton followed Bahve, a disciple of Gandhi. Apparently, Drayton, referring to Bahve, once claimed: 'I saw him as a living saint. Today I would probably see him as a social entrepreneur' (Drayton, quoted in Bornstein, 2007: 53). The centrality of individuals' exceptional character is complemented by the marginality of issues related to governance, legal status and the role of governments as well as of the market. Alex Nicholls, in the introduction of One of the first and more complete edited books on social entrepreneurship, *Social Entrepreneurship New Models of Sustainable Change*, makes this clear when he asserts that 'social entrepreneurs and their networks demonstrate an unrelenting focus on systemic social change that disregards institutional and organizational norms and boundaries' (Nicholls, 2006: 10). An excerpt from the Ashoka website underlines the same point, focusing on the ability of social entrepreneurs to bypass both public and private sectors, to finally find those 'solutions' that nobody had found before:

> Rather than leaving societal needs to the government or business sectors, social entrepreneurs find what is not working and solve the problem by changing the

> system, spreading the solution, and persuading entire societies to take new leaps. . . . Social entrepreneurs often seem to be possessed by their ideas, committing their lives to changing the direction of their field. They are both visionaries and ultimate realists, concerned with the practical implementation of their vision above all else.
>
> (Ashoka, 2016c)

What distinguishes social entrepreneurs for these authors is exactly this power of ideas – the 'vision' – over the stiff mechanisms of bureaucratic government and the purpose-less activities of the private sector. These 'innovative' ideas can potentially take any possible form, any form of governance, any legal status, they can be part of any possible field of activity. Michael Young, British founder of the Young Foundation and a significant figure in the scene, states that:

> what is new and most distinctive about social entrepreneurship is not the particular organizational forms that are used but the entrepreneur's continual pursuit of greater social or environmental impact.
>
> (Young, 2006: 59)

Young reiterates the flexibility of social entrepreneurship as a field of action, whereby the organisational forms are not rigidly defined or fixed. Instead, these remarks focus on the individual's inspired activity – their 'continual pursuit' of something greater. To run a social enterprise is not even so much about partaking in a specific set of practices, but being a certain kind of person, with a certain kind of inspiration. Dees asserts that social entrepreneurs do not even necessarily run a business (Dees, 1998). He claims social entrepreneurs explore all resource options, from pure philanthropy to the commercial methods of the business sector; and they are not bound by sector norms or traditions (Dees, 1998: 5). This being outside 'norms and tradition' is typical of charismatic authority, which 'by contrast to all sorts of bureaucratic or official organization . . . knows nothing of a form or of a regular procedure'. (Weber, 2009: 246)

Attempts have been made to attenuate the individualistic perspective of these views (see, for instance, Collaborative Changemaking: Oxford innovation Communities Project, launched in 2013 and supported by the Skoll Centre), or at least to avoid a heroic narrative (Nicholls, 2013). Dey and Steyaert also critique this tendency, and deconstruct what they identify as the 'grand narrative' of social entrepreneurship: a dominant discourse that 'presents social change as a harmonious process relying on a messianic script' (Dey and Steyaert, 2010: 88). EMES takes a different tact, conceptualising social entrepreneurship as a collective, community based endeavour (Defourny and Nyssens, 2010), in open opposition to individualistic accounts that 'reflect a shift towards focusing on individuals and away from traditional emphasis on the community and collective, found in community development and the co-op movement'. (Grenier, 2003: 4)

Light (2006) is another prominent supporter of a more community-centric perspective. He criticises Ashoka's definition of social entrepreneurs – that is, 'individuals with the committed vision and inexhaustible determination to persist until they have transformed the entire system' and who 'go beyond the immediate problem to fundamentally change communities, societies, and the world' (Ashoka, quoted in Light, 2006: 48) – arguing that:

> By focusing so much on visionary change agents, prominent advocates of social entrepreneurship have excluded large numbers of organizations that deserve the financial support, networking, and training now reserved for individuals who fit both the current definition of social entrepreneurship and the prevailing model of the self-sacrificing entrepreneur.
>
> (Light: 2006: 48)

Light's position is understandable. Not only does such a vision risk exclusion through skewed self-selection (what kind of person thinks they qualify?), it surely also undermines Gordon's (2016) claim that social entrepreneurs can expect to 'live lives of relative comfort', due to the immense burdens placed upon them. Yet, these attempts to draw a profile of the social entrepreneur as a contemporary hero are of great interest from the perspective of cultural studies. Indeed, any ideal type, any mythical character, however unrealistic or exaggerated, and even theoretically or morally wrong, reveals a mode of thinking, a vision of how the world should be. It also offers insight into the lived experience of becoming an entrepreneur: the expectations, the self-doubt and the need to cultivate a certain kind of subjectivity. As we begin to encounter the aspiring social entrepreneurs that will provide our window onto this world – people like Alfredo, Anita and Sara – we will see just how these kinds of mythic qualities are interpreted and experienced by real individuals. This book can therefore be understood as an empirical investigation into the idealised social entrepreneur, an exploration of how certain discourses of social entrepreneurship and social entrepreneurs are embodied and enacted by flesh and bone individuals.

A SITE OF SUBJECTIVATION

By conceptualising social entrepreneurship's modes of governance in Weberian terms as bureaucratic and charismatic, it's possible to account for the material basis for the mythic narrative that pervades social entrepreneurship.

Rather than regulating the enterprise, charismatic governance seeks to regulate the entrepreneur. Through a narrative of heroic integrity and invincible inspiration, the social entrepreneur is expected to behave properly – to both know and do the right thing – when the twin imperatives of making money and doing good come into conflict.

Entrepreneurs have long been conceived as exceptional individuals with the capacity to enact radical change through combining multiple fields of action. Since its earliest formulation by Jean Baptiste Say in the 19th century (1821), entrepreneurship has been characterised by its ability to connect and combine different orders of value and logics of thinking and acting. The entrepreneur is a creative subject defined by his or her ability to operate new combinations, which are not the result of a gradual and consequential development of existing conditions, but rather are originated by means of a quantum jump (Schumpeter, 1989). This should not be interpreted as a form of personalism: what is at stake is an abstract process – a 'mechanism', but which unfolds in actual societies by means of individual actions. The individual functions as 'the bearer of the *mechanism of change*' (Schumpeter, 1989: 61, emphasis in the original).

Indeed, to account for entrepreneurs' force of 'creative destruction', Schumpeter coined the term 'Unternehmergeist', literally: the entrepreneurial spirit. The introduction of a spirit – that is, something, transcendent, which exceeds calculative reason – at the heart of economic theory opens the room for a reflection on economy as a human enterprise marked by risk, creativity and unexpected turns. Postulating the unpredictable and creative human agency at the base of economic development, Schumpeterian theory connects the social and human dimensions to the economic, breaking with a mainstream thinking that treats economics as a fully autonomous discipline, independent and separable from the whole of human activities.[1]

This inspirational character is at the core of contemporary social entrepreneurship's discourses. Put differently, at the core of social entrepreneurship is a particular kind of subject. They are described as exceptional change agents; a 'rare breed' (Dees, 2001: 4), who are 'possessed by their ideas' (Ashoka, 2017), and able to 'persuade entire societies to take new leaps' (Drayton, quoted in Kois, 2013: 188). Social entrepreneurs can well be thought of as agents who wholeheartedly actualise the Schumpeterian entrepreneurial spirit.

Yet, differently from Schumpeter's entrepreneurs, social entrepreneurship's discourses portray social entrepreneurs as exceptional individuals who not only enact a spirit of history that exists before, in a logical and ontological sense, but make history happen. They are depicted as self-aware actors who claim the right and power to 'forge' the spirit of history and to consciously produce it. Furthermore, most of the times they are described as fiercely opposed to corporate and institutional culture. In this regard, the human agency that Schumpeter put at the core of his theory of entrepreneurship at a phenomenological and historical level (individuals actualise principles whose origin is beyond their agency and will) becomes an 'ontological' feature of social entrepreneurs' subjectivity, an attribute that defines their very being. Social entrepreneurship can therefore also be understood as a field of subjectivation – a site where a particular kind of subjectivity is fashioned.

The question we initially set out – what is social entrepreneurship? – therefore begs another: Who is the social entrepreneur? That is, what kind of subject is the social entrepreneur, and how do they create themselves? To answer this, we must first situate the social entrepreneur within the wider context of neoliberalism in which they have arisen. By pinpointing the peculiarity of the social entrepreneur as a subject, we will be able to explore some of the characters that mark the spirit of contemporary capitalism in Western societies. In particular, we will see how a fully individualised subject attempts to retrieve an ethical and political dimension, thereby claiming the right and desire to change how things are. This will lead to a reflection on the specific forms of ethics and politics that may be at stake in this enterprise.

NOTE

1. This connection emerges clearly in the very first pages of the second chapter of the *Theory of Economic Developments*: 'Economic development is so far simply the object of economic history, which in turn is merely a part of a universal history, only separated from the rest for purposes of exposition. Because of this fundamental dependence of the economic aspect of things on everything else it is not possible to explain economic change on the basis of economic conditions alone. For the economic state of a people does not emerge simply from the preceding economic conditions, but only from the preceding total situation' (Schumpeter, 1989: 58).

Chapter II

Neoliberalism and the Entrepreneurialisation of the Self

Social entrepreneurs are individuals who express their ethical and political values and virtues – that is, the will to 'change the world' – through work. Rather than a site of drudgery or boredom, work is understood as a medium through which to perform these values, to express a particular kind of ethical self. The notion of expressing an aspirational self through work, of which social entrepreneurship is the extreme iteration, has its roots in the emergence of neoliberalism. In this chapter, we will trace how the self came to be understood as expressed through work by drawing on Foucault's account of 'the entrepreneur of the self' as a wider observation of neoliberalism's recombination of multiple domains of action – namely, the economic and the existential. We will then draw on a range of literature exploring the manifold ways in which neoliberalism demands the investment of the self – the soul, even – in One's work, FOR the philosophical core of neoliberalism previously thought to be non-economic' (Foucault, 2010: 221).

As we will see more in depth in the following chapters, social entrepreneurs are individuals who express their values and virtues by means of work, hence giving an economic interpretation to ethical and political sentiments. In this regard, they bear the core traits of neoliberal subjectivities. However, while it may be tempting to disregard the social entrepreneur as passively co-opted into neoliberal regimes of governmentality, we must resist such a straightforward reading. Like all subjects in any society, they are individuals with agency, they reflexively negotiate opportunities and constraints and they attempt to live and enact their values through the means available to them. In this chapter, I want to explore these tensions, by highlighting both the neoliberal origin of social entrepreneurship, and the extent to which it might challenge neoliberal governmentality.

NEOLIBERALISM AND THE ENTREPRENEUR

In *The Birth of Biopolitics*, a series of lectures given at the *Collège de France* in 1978–1979, Michel Foucault traces a genealogy of neoliberal governmentality that, starting from the recognition of neoliberal political economy as a principle of limitation of the power of the state, indicates the production of an entrepreneurial society and subjectivity as its logical outcomes. It is striking that, almost three decades ago, the French philosopher and historian had already grasped the significance that the category of the enterprise will have acquired in every aspect of life. Foucault's analysis, though preceding the rise of social enterprises, can help trace the neoliberal origins of social entrepreneurship.

According to Foucault, neoliberalism is characterised by a conception of the market as a system whose conditions of efficiency have to be constantly produced. For this reason, neoliberal governmentality differs from liberal governmentality, which in its declination of laissez-faire, and since the Physiocrats, was rooted in the view of the market as a 'natural mechanism' that the state only had to supervise and control. For the liberals, the natural functioning of the market was supposed to be based on 'exchange', an activity among equal partners, and regulated by the self-ruling mechanism of prices. Quite differently, neoliberalism understands the market as regulated by competition (Foucault, 2010: 118).

Competition is not a 'natural given': on the contrary, it is a dynamic that needs to be constantly produced and reproduced. To conceive of the market as based on competition implies thinking of it as constantly changing and evolving and therefore in need of input from the social sphere. It follows that the role of governmental reason should be that of producing, at the level of the social, the conditions for the market to function. As Donzelot puts it: 'The role of the State is to intervene in favour of the market rather than because of the market, in such a way that the market is always maintained and that the principle of equal inequality produces its effect' (Donzelot, 2008: 124). In other words, since the market is thought of as rooted in the mechanism of competition, laissez-faire is not an option any more.

Foucault's elaboration of this point is worth quoting in full:

> Competition has an internal logic; it has its own structure. Its effects are only produced if this logic is respected. It is, as it were, a formal game between inequalities; it is not a natural game between individuals and behaviors. . . . This means that pure competition is not a primitive given. It can only be the result of lengthy efforts and, in truth, pure competition is never attained. Pure competition must and can only be an objective, an objective thus presupposing

> an indefinitely active policy. Competition is therefore a historical objective of governmental art and not a natural given that must be respected.
>
> (Foucault, 2010: 120)

The social is no longer seen as a remedy for the inequalities caused by the market, rather it becomes the very 'factory' of inequalities, the 'historical objective' of governmental art, which must create the formal and material condition of inequalities so that competition can be produced and reproduced. As Donzelot put it: 'social policy is no longer a means for countering the economic, but a means to sustain the logic of competition'. (Donzelot, 2008: 124)

Foucault identifies 'entrepreneurship' as the building block of this competitiveness. The regulation and organisation of a society that is able to produce successful conditions for the competitive market to function finds in the 'enterprise' its basic unit. Competition is based on the manufacturing of freedom, albeit a particular type of freedom, the freedom to organise and manage resources so as to be well equipped to partake in the 'formal game of inequalities'. Such freedom is an entrepreneurial freedom, the liberty to acquire the capabilities of using resources so as to actualise projects in an autonomous and financially sustainable way. The enterprise is the form of this freedom: freedom to compete and to capitalise on One's skills, talents, passions and so on.

THE ENTREPRENEUR OF THE SELF

The subject that epitomises, embodies and enacts this mode of neoliberal economy is, for Foucault, 'the entrepreneur of the self'. Foucault deduces and discusses the figure of the entrepreneur of the self through the analysis of Gary Becker's notion of human capital, in which he sees the most exhaustive disclosure of neoliberal philosophy. He claims that American neoliberalism, which finds in the concept of human capital One its most comprehensive expressions, enacts an 'absolute generalization' of 'the form of the market' (Foucault, 2010: 243). From here, it is possible to trace the emergence of the entrepreneur as investing and articulating a particular kind of self, as much as a particular model for running a business. In other words, it is possible to trace the origins of the social entrepreneur.

For Foucault, what the idea of human capital implies is to look at labour from the point of view of the worker. This is the fundamental perspective shift of Becker's theory, and of neoliberalism in general, for it recognises labour as a practice, and the worker as an active economic subject. The neoliberals insist on this point, Foucault argues, charging both classical and Marxist economic theories as considering labour only in terms of quantity and price.

Instead, they suggest regarding it as an activity in which workers use their skills to get an income. Within this conceptual framework, an individual's set of abilities – manual, cognitive, technical and creative – is conceived of as human capital: they are 'human' for they are inseparable from the person who possesses them, and they are deployed as a form of capital since it is by putting them to work that the worker gets an income. From the viewpoint of the worker, then, income is a return on investment of the self. This way of deciphering work implies a reconceptualisation of workers' subjectivity for they are required to think of themselves as possessing certain attributes that have to be managed in a profitable way. Therefore 'the worker appears as a sort of enterprise for himself [*sic*]' (Foucault, 2010: 225), embodying the form of life of a *homo economicus* as the entrepreneur of the self:

> *homo economicus* is an entrepreneur, an entrepreneur of himself. This is true to the extent that, in practice, the stake in all neoliberal analyses is the replacement every time of *homo economicus* as partner of exchange with a *homo economicus* as entrepreneur of himself, being for himself his own capital, being for himself his own producer, being for himself the source of his earnings.
>
> (Foucault, 2010: 226)

At stake is a redefinition of the meaning and objective of One's life and identity, since it is One's own life to be deciphered through the category of the enterprise. The individual life is thereby conceived as a 'permanent and multiple enterprise' (Foucault, 2010: 241). Each skill, thought, desire and passion can possibly become – they must become – the 'material' of the enterprise, something that can be put to work. The self becomes an investable quality, and its monetary return becomes the litmus test of One's value. At play is an absolute generalisation of the form of the enterprise:

American neoliberalism still involves, in fact, the generalization of the economic form of the market. It involves generalizing it throughout the social body and including the whole of the social system not usually conducted through or sanctioned by monetary exchanges (Foucault, 2010: 243).The enterprise's ability to describe both an economic, rational action, and a quasi-spiritual, heroic, human endeavour, thereby makes it a suitable category for the conjunction of an economic dimension within the social, ethical and political spheres.

Here the category of the enterprise functions as a sort of Kantian schema that translates the domain of the economy into that of the self, turning the first into a form of capital, and the latter into a self-actualising and self-producing activity. Indeed, it could be argued that the philosophical core of neoliberalism, which is fully embedded in the notion of enterprise and in its various declinations, for example, entrepreneurial market, self and society, is the 'possibility of giving a strictly economic interpretation of a whole domain previously thought to be non-economic' (Foucault, 2010: 221). The entrepreneur of the self is the subject for whom the translation of the self into a form of business shall spontaneously follow from the very perception of their being. An entrepreneurialised subjectivity can be thus described as that for which competition and uncertainty, investment and profit, are not only economic but also existential categories. For the entrepreneur of the self, *res oeconomica* and *res existentialis* fully coincide.

THE SELF AT WORK

In the past three decades, a significant number of studies have explored the implications and effects of entrepreneurialisation of the self and work in neoliberal societies (e.g. DuGay, 1996; Sennett, 1998; Thrift, 1998, 2005; Adkins and Lury, 1999; McRobbie, 2001, 2002, 2015; Ross, 2004; Gill and Pratt, 2008). What emerges from these accounts is the shifting meaning of work. Previously perceived as the site of alienation, of repetitive tasks to be performed with no personal investment, work has been redefined and reorganised as 'part of that continuum along which "we" all seek to realize ourselves as particular sets of person-outcomes, self-regulatory, self-fulfilling individual actors' (Thrift, 2005: 34).

Work is perceived as something creative, and passionate (McRobbie, 1997, 2001, 2002; Arvidsson et al., 2010). Angela McRobbie observes that for some sections of the population, it 'has become an important source for self-actualization, even freedom and independence' (McRobbie, 2002: 518); and aptly notes that 'there is a utopian thread embedded in this wholehearted attempt to make-over the world of work into something closer to a life of enthusiasm and enjoyment' (McRobbie, 2002: 521). Paul DuGay argues that this 'humanisation' of the workplace has been central to the endeavour of management scholars in the past five decades, their concern being how to effectively encourage employees to work autonomously, take responsibilities and develop problem-solving skills while acting in the interest of the firm (DuGay, 1996). As he put it, regardless of the differences between different schools of thought, management scholars have been united by a focus on 'the production and regulation of particular work-based subjectivities' (DuGay, 1996: 59).

The core of the managerial shift revolved around making the self a space of intervention, something to be produced in accordance with the needs of the company. Employees started to be encouraged to express themselves, to be independent, to engage in activities of self-assessment and reciprocal feed-back (Newton, 1995). In the most successful cases, they are seen as providing valuable inputs, catalysing innovative practices and spreading their charisma, for the benefit of the company. In other words, they adopt an entrepreneurial conduct within their role as dependent worker. As DuGay, drawing on Rose (1989, 1990) and Gordon (1987), puts it: 'Excellent companies seek to cultivate enterprising subjects – autonomous, self-regulating, productive individuals' (DuGay, 1996: 60).

The fashioning of the self becomes part of the tasks to be fulfilled at work. In this respect, the process of self-fashioning, far from being a spontaneous act of self-expression, resembles more a set of skills that must be learnt and deployed. Indeed, as Lazzarato put it, 'To be employable One must conduct oneself and have a lifestyle which is in harmony with the market' (Lazzarato, 2009: 127). In such context, 'being oneself' becomes a command, instead of a principle of freedom. One's lifestyle and identity – if in harmony with the market needs – can become a unique selling proposition of the entrepreneurialised worker (Bandinelli, 2019). This process of commodification of the self has been encapsulated in practices and discourse around self-branding: One's brand serves as a device for the management and communication of One's identity and value in the job market (Hearn, 2011; Bandinelli and Arvidsson, 2013; Marwick, 2013; Arvidsson et al., 2016). At the same time, the failure to own, promote and sell – in One word: to brand – One's identity, can cause One's exclusion from or marginalisation in the job market (see, for instance, Adkins and Lury [2006] for a gender perspective on this matter).[1]

Upon closer inspection, being oneself is a formula that entails the production and performance of a specific self, that is, the entrepreneurial self. As Rose puts it: 'The enterprising self will make a venture of its life, project itself a future and seek to shape itself in order to become that which it wishes to be' (Rose, 1990: 6). One substantial feature of the entrepreneurial subjectivity is precisely an understanding of the self as something to be fashioned: Entrepreneurs of the self must be able to reform and perform his or her identities continuously and in accordance with the changing environment of the neoliberal flexible and casualised job market (DuGay, 1996; Sennet, 1998; Adkins and Lury, 2006).

Post-Operaists scholars have stressed the exploitative character of the entrepreneurialisation of the self. Since the self is what needs to be produced within the capitalist system, it becomes subsumed into its logic (Lazzarato, 1996; Virno, 2005; Berardi, 2009). Maurizio Lazzarato, in his analysis of Post-Fordist labour, argues that self-expression is the very basis of capital exploitation. As he puts it, what modern management techniques are looking for is for the worker's soul to become part of the factory. The worker's personality and subjectivity have to be made susceptible to organisation and command (Lazzarato, 1996: 133).

This theorisation elucidates both movements of expression and exploitation. The subject becomes the core of production in as much as it is a unique subject, with a unique 'soul': there is hence a process of valorisation of the self, of self-valorisation. However, since the subject has to produce value within a capitalist economy, their expression must be subjugated and commanded. The entrepreneurialised subject is then caught in an ambivalent condition, occupying the position of both their own manager and slave, being 'capitalist and proletarian' at the same time (Lazzarato, drawing on Deleuze and Guattari, 2009: 126).

BETWEEN GOVERNANCE AND SELF-EXPRESSION

Social entrepreneurs would appear to exemplify this opportunity, as they are able to combine the necessity of work with the autonomy of ethical self-expression. Their ambition is to not only make money, but do what they believe to be good. In this sense, social entrepreneurs replicate the traits of workers in the culture industries: they conceive their work as the primary medium for self-expression, and embrace the belief that work can become a source of pleasure and enjoyment. The 'utopian thread' indicated by McRobbie seems to be even more evident in social entrepreneurs' narratives, which make of work the way to improve not only personal lives but also society as such.

However, they also exemplify the willingness to pay a significant price for this luxury. As Lazzarato notes, contemporary workers operate in 'an economic space in which individuals individually take upon themselves and confront risks' (Lazzarato, 2009: 118). The imperative of being an entrepreneur of the self, while it is felt as empowering in so far as it allows a high degree of independence, implies that One is obliged to take all the risks and responsibilities for the success or failure of their career (McRobbie, 1998, 2002; Sennett, 1998; Bauman, 2000, 2006; Ross, 2004, 2008; Arvidsson et al., 2010). The risk-taking nature of social entrepreneurship – perhaps even riskier than enterprises that are concerned with only with financial sustainability – is celebrated within its discourse of exceptionalism but entails enormous vulnerability. And, in the name of passion and ethics, social entrepreneurs accept the renunciation of any form of welfare, security or even (as is often the case) a workplace with consistent colleagues. Such de-spatialisation, coupled with the absence of traditional institutions such as trade unions, may reflect the depoliticization of work typical of neoliberal societies.

The concept of the entrepreneurial self – with its corollary of freedom and self-actualisation – produces a self-employed, self-exploiting workforce, composed of individual workers who, practically deprived of collective forms of political organisation and representation (e.g. trade unions), existentially collapsed into their own individuality and emotionally marked by precariousness and anxiety, have provided the necessary labour power for an increasingly deregulated and casualised work environment (McRobbie, 2001, 2002; Ross, 2004, 2008; Christopherson, 2008). Overall, values of solidarity and social justice have been overlooked or dismissed in favour of an exaltation of individuality articulated in the narratives of ambition and success, which have been the soundtrack of the culture industry both in the US and UK (McRobbie, 2001, 2002; Gill and Pratt, 2008; Ross, 2008). 'Maybe', McRobbie argues, 'there can be no workplace politics when there is no workplace' (McRobbie, 2002: 521–522).

The euphoric discourse surrounding social entrepreneurship could therefore be interpreted as merely ideological, and analysed in so far as it subsumes the social into a mode of the economic. It could also be argued that social entrepreneurship is nothing more than a brand to glamourize a post-welfare social policy that attempts to reorganise the public sector as a network of individual, localised and financially autonomous enterprises, bringing to the extreme what Beck described as the tendency to find 'biographical' solutions to systemic and structural problems (Beck, 1997). Yet, even if all of this was uncontrovertibly true, we would still be witnessing the attempt on the part of a fully individualised neoliberal subject to explicitly re-embed an ethical, social and political dimension.

As we will see through the course of this book, social entrepreneurs claim to be driven by the need to positively impact on society, and do not perceive their entrepreneurial activities as an obstacle, but rather as the most adequate means to pursue this objective. In this respect, social entrepreneurs enact a specific subjectivity that does not fully coincide with that of the entrepreneur of the self, for it reintegrates – at least discursively – social justice and solidarity with individualism and entrepreneurialism. In a sense, they are entrepreneurs of the self who value other achievements besides profit.

Dismissing the phenomenon as yet another form of capital cooptation would therefore prevent an analysis of the specificities of the social entrepreneurship discourse, ultimately leading to the tautological argument that people living in neoliberal societies act and think in neoliberal ways. Instead, the objective of this book is to delve into the paradoxical character of a fully individualised entrepreneur of the self who acts for the collective good in a neoliberal society, where the collective good is supposedly invisible (Foucault, 2010: 282) and where individuals are in structural competition with each other. In this respect, I aim at offering a critique of social entrepreneurship which is not reducible to a 'fault-finding' (Williams, quoted in Butler, 2002: 1) practice or to the objective of formulating a judgement. On the contrary, it moves exactly from the suspension of judgement as a methodological premise to open the space for a practice of analytical understanding (Butler,

2002). For these reasons, the pages that follow will be led by the question of how neoliberal subjects can reintegrate in a social, ethical and political dimension, and what such processes imply and exclude. In other words, it will focus on the subjective viewpoint of social entrepreneurs to explore how they actualise; enact; make sense of and think about the re-embedding of a social, ethical and political dimension within their entrepreneurial practices.

To account for this dialectical relation between freedom and power, it is useful to turn again to Foucault. In his last works, he stresses the fact that technologies of power are always in relation to 'technologies of the self', and the notion of governmentality is to be found at the crossroads of these two (Foucault, 2000). This means that individuals are always in the process of negotiating and confronting, as well as reproducing and enacting, instances of power. One should then resist the temptation to dismiss every individualised subject as a passive product of neoliberal governmentality. In this respect, I maintain Angela McRobbie's warning against a too-simplistic intellectual manoeuvre that collapses individualisation into neoliberal governmentality (McRobbie, 2001). It is the complex intertwining of emancipation and exploitation, freedom and cooptation, and passion and anxieties, which marks contemporary neoliberal subjects, and social entrepreneurs exemplify precisely this character. Understanding social entrepreneurs offers, I want to suggest, a unique prism through which to understand contemporary society.

SOCIAL ENTREPRENEURS' SUBJECTIVITY AND REGIME OF TRUTH

To conduct an enquiry into the social entrepreneur, I employ the Foucauldian categories of 'regime of truth' and 'process of subjectivation'. These two interrelated concepts offer the opportunity to think both in abstract and in empirical terms, for their relationship highlights the correspondence between subscribing to a certain mode of thinking and becoming a certain kind of subject. In the 1977 interview, 'The Political Function of the Intellectual', Michel Foucault explains that the expression 'regime of truth' means a number of related things: (1) 'the types of discourse [society] harbours and causes to function as true'; (2) 'the mechanisms and instances which enable One to distinguish true from false statement' and (3) 'the way in which each is sanctioned'; (4) 'the techniques and procedures which are valorised for obtaining truth'; (5) 'the status of those who are charged with saying what counts as true' (Foucault, 1977, p. 12–13).

While I do not follow these prescriptions in an orthodox manner, I do take the concept of regime of truth to indicate that a given mode of thinking is constructed over some basic assumptions that, while rarely expressed, constitute the foundation of a certain vision of the world. Analysing the regime of truth of social entrepreneurship involves exploring the assumptions on which it is built. It involves asking the simple but essential questions: What vision of the social and the entrepreneurial is implied in something like a 'social enterprise'? What vision of 'change' is implied in social entrepreneurs' claims of 'changing the world'? What notion of ethics is at stake in the 'doing good' of social entrepreneurship? In a nutshell, it means exploring how social entrepreneurship is thinkable. In a sense, I use the notion of regime of truth in as much as it offers an analytical methodology, that is, it functions as a frame to indicate a certain approach to the topic.

The same applies to the notion of subjectivity. With this concept, I want to indicate the fact that thinking certain thoughts makes of someone a certain person. This is to say that those who embrace the regime of truth of social entrepreneurship become social entrepreneurial subjects. In his *On the Government of The Living: Lectures at the Collège de France, 1979–1980*, Foucault argues that the acceptance of a regime of truth is related to a process of subjectivation. Since I accept (*je m'incline*) a regime of truth, I self-qualify in a certain way, constituting myself as a specific subject, by means of the application of a number of technologies of the self (Foucault, 2014). As Lorenzini puts it: 'This acceptance takes the form of a subjection (*assujettissement*) or of a subjectivation (subjectivation), since every regime of truth asks the individuals who are implicated in it for a specific self-constitution' (Lorenzini, 2013: 3).

This focus on the self is particularly appropriate for the analysis of a phenomenon in which the stress on a particular subject – the social entrepreneur – is so prominent. Moreover, it permits to approach the analysis of social entrepreneurship's regime of truth not in abstract terms, but rather to pinpoint its embodied nature, the modes by which it is enacted, spoken and produced by living individuals. Indeed, although Foucault has never conducted empirical, ethnographic research, his analytical methodology can well be applied to living, embodied subjects. In this regard, this research resonates with Ian Hacking's purpose of combining Foucault 'top-down', 'pure descriptions of discursive events' – with the actual speakers, or writers, 'left out or presented only by implication' – with Goffman 'bottom-up' interests in 'concrete conversations' between embodied individuals (Hacking, 2004: 278). Even if I do not draw specifically on Goffman himself, I do combine a Foucauldian theoretical framework and analytical methodology with ethnography. At stake, there is the attempt to bring Foucault 'down to the self'.

This is not an isolated attempt. Besides Hacking, this type of research has been carried out by the anthropologists of ethics. Starting from Foucault's definition of ethics as a process of subjectivation, anthropologists of ethics have pursued ethnographic research to investigate how individuals constitute themselves as particular subjects (see, for instance, Faubion, 2001, 2011; Laidlaw, 2002; Pandian, 2010). In the last years of his life and research, Michel Foucault closely explored the means, ends and significance of the process through which individuals create themselves as subjects, tracing its origin back to the ancient Greek notion and practices of *epimeleia heautou*, the care of the self (Foucault, 2005). As he stated in a 1983 interview, this intellectual endeavour can be thought of as a 'genealogy of ethics' (Foucault, 2000: 266) where the term 'ethics' refers to 'the kind of relationship you ought to be with yourself, *rapport a sòi*' (Foucault, 2000: 263). Therefore, ethics – regardless of the particular moral systems that may originate from it in different historical contexts – is a form of continual work on the self, a perennial activity of 'self bricolage' (Rabinow, 2000: xxxix). As Laidlaw aptly notices, this concept of ethics is far 'wider than the following of socially sanctioned moral rules', for it 'includes our response to invitations or injunctions to make oneself into a certain kind of person' (Laidlaw, 2002: 321–22).

The diverse dispositives which 'permit individuals to effect by their own means, or with the help of others, a certain number of operations on their own bodies and souls, conduct, and way of being, so as to transform themselves in order to attain a certain state' are named by Foucault 'technologies of the self' (Foucault, 2000: 225). Technologies of the self are those with which the individual can 'act upon himself [*sic*]' (Foucault, 1988: 16). As such, they necessarily produce an ethos, they are *ethopoios*, which means that they 'possess the quality of transforming ethos' (Foucault, 2005: 237).

Importantly, this notion of ethics as a project of self-fashioning unfolds between the two extremes of freedom and domination: individuals exercise their freedom by effecting operations so as to transform and craft themselves, through processes of subjectivation, but these practices of the self 'are nevertheless not something invented by the individual himself [*sic*]. They are models that he finds in his culture and that are proposed, suggested, imposed upon him by his culture, his society his social group' (Foucault, 2000: 291). To put it another way, processes of subjectivation unfold always in relation to 'games of truth' and 'practices of power' (Foucault, 2000: 290). Therefore, the kind of freedom exercised by the ethical subject is never of an absolute kind, rather it is defined by a web of power relationships and regimes of truth.

It is at the crossroads of technologies of domination and technologies of the self that Foucault individuates the field for the study of governmentality (Foucault, 2000: 225). As explained by Agamben, 'Processes of subjectivation bring the individual to bind himself to his [*sic*] own identity and consciousness and, at the same time, to an external power' (Agamben, 1998: 5).

This implies that the subject is never a stable, simple, substance, but rather a composite form that is not 'always identical to itself':

> You do not have the same type of relationship to yourself when you constitute yourself as a political subject . . . and when you are seeking to fulfil your desires in a sexual relationship. Undoubtedly there are relationship and interferences between these different forms of the subject; but we are not dealing with the same type of subject. In each case, One plays, One establishes a different type of relationship to oneself.
>
> (Foucault, 2000: 290)

Drawing on this parlance, the following pages can be read as an attempt to analyse the relationship that some embodied individuals establish with themselves in so far as they constitute themselves as 'social entrepreneurs'. Doing that implies analysing how they produce and are produced by the social entrepreneurship regime of truth. Such an analytical toolkit has at least two great advantages. Firstly, it creates the space for analysis that does not collapse into the neoliberal dominance of individuals' thoughts and actions. To put it another way, it permits us to affect an analysis at the crossroads between power and resistance. Secondly, in so far as it allows to explore the process of self-constitution, it provides a method with which to approach the production of subjectivity that characterises work in neoliberal societies, in this case, to tackle the question 'How do individuals constitute themselves as social entrepreneurial subjects?'.

In short, the objective of this book is to decipher and analyse the discursive and material procedures and techniques that are mobilised so as to produce social entrepreneurship as a sphere of thoughts and actions that create truths and subjectivities. As I will show, the regime of truth produced by social entrepreneurship involves specific conceptions of sociality, ethics and politics.

SOCIALITY, ETHICS AND POLITICS IN SOCIAL ENTREPRENEURSHIP

Exploring and articulating the meaning of sociality, ethics and politics within the discourse of social entrepreneurship will be the objective of the remainder of this book. That said, at this stage, I want to offer provisional definitions as reference points for what follows. Let me clarify that I use the terms 'sociality', 'ethics' and 'politics' as heuristic devices. This is to say that rather than providing a positive definition, they delimit a field of enquiry, functioning as benchmarks around which variations and differences can be situated. Indeed, the aim of my research is precisely that of deducing the notions of ethics, sociality and politics at stake in social entrepreneurs discourse and practices. For these reasons, they will acquire a more concrete meaning over the following chapters. For now, I just offer a synthetic description of the field of enquiry that they indicate.

With the term 'sociality', I broadly refer to the characters and functions that human interaction acquires in a specific context. In particular, I draw on studies of sociality at work to investigate the meaning that social interactions acquire in the sphere of work (Lazzarato, 1997; Wittel, 2001; Gregg, 2007, 2011; Marwick, 2013). Therefore, an analysis of social entrepreneurs' sociality can be seen as a case study of the impact, scope and significance of social interactions in the organisation of work for entrepreneurialised subjects operating in neoliberal economies and society. More specifically, it concerns the issue of social entrepreneurs' re-integration of a social dimension in their discourse and practices.

In this book, the signifier 'social' is used in three interrelated meanings. The first refers to a cultural discourse around the activity of certain individuals who identify themselves as social entrepreneurs: individuals whose declared objective is to tackle social issues by means of the enterprise. In other words, it is the label 'social' attached to the 'enterprise', and it indicates the topic of this study. The second refers to the organisation of work in neoliberal societies, which is rooted on the production and exploitation of social relationships (Lazzarato, 1996, 2009; Hardt and Negri, 1999; Wittel, 2001; Gregg, 2007, 2011). In this sense, the term 'social' indicates a specific understanding of the neoliberal organisation of work and refers to a certain literature, which I will further discuss in chapter IV. The third relates to the specific sociality of social entrepreneurs, the features of which emerge from the analysis of ethnographic data proposed in chapter IV. As stated earlier, the sociality of social entrepreneurs can be seen as an instantiation of the broader assimilation of work and social relationships typical of neoliberal modes of value production.

I use the term 'ethics' to refer to two intermingled dimensions. The first concerns a value horizon against which individuals assess their actions and thoughts to the extent that these are adequate for the pursuit of maximum collective happiness. As can be noticed, this definition echoes Aristotle's notion of ethics as *eudaimonia*, which he develops in the *Nicomachean Ethics*. Importantly, this is not a prescriptive definition, for example, it is not concerned with specific norms of conduct that point at a specific morality.

Rather, it concerns the analysis of the values and virtues that can lead to living a good life with others. Following this, I define an investigation of social entrepreneurs ethics as an analysis of how they reintegrate a collective dimension within an entrepreneurialised and individualised subjectivity. The second is the Foucauldian meaning that I have discussed in the previous section: it involves the processes of subjectivations in which individuals embark so as to make of themselves a certain subject. In this latter meaning, ethics is a hermeneutic of the self.

The meaning of politics that I use in this book exceeds the domain of the state, and looks at the analysis of 'what we are willing to accept in our world – to accept, to refuse, to change – both in ourselves and in our circumstances' (Foucault, 2007: 152). Drawing on Foucault, I conceive of politics as the dimension of discourses and actions that involve the will to act in order to alter the order of things, to impact and improve on the ways in which society is structured, organised and managed. Hannah Arendt's definition of political discourse and actions is helpful to further specify this concept of politics. According to the German theorist, politics has to do with the discourse and actions dealing with change, with the future and therefore with the unforeseeable and unpredictable (Arendt, 1998). At stake is an anthropological notion of politics that concerns individuals' political feelings, thoughts and actions. Within this framework, analysing social entrepreneurs' politics represents an attempt to understand the significance of the notion of 'change' that they mobilise, and how this is redefined by its intertwining with the form of the enterprise.

CONCLUSION

Social entrepreneurs embody a type of subjectivity that does not fully coincide with that of the entrepreneur of the self described by Foucault (2010) and by many critical scholars after him (e.g. Lazzarato, 2009; and McNay, 2009). Indeed, while operating in a neoliberal society and economy and fostering a highly individualised conduct – the entrepreneurial conduct – they seek to have a 'positive impact' on society, to 'make a change'. However vague the words 'change' and 'impact' may be – I will explore this matter in the following chapters – they signal the attempt to reconcile – at least discursively – entrepreneurialism and social responsibility. To this extent, social entrepreneurship may represent a socio-cultural formation characterised by an inherently ambivalent position in relation to the neoliberal political economy, and an augmentation of the entrepreneur of the self. We will seek to explore and problematise such ambivalence, by analysing the forms in which social entrepreneurship discourse integrates entrepreneurialism, therefore an individualising and competitive conduct, with the quest for social justice. How can entrepreneurialised and individualised subjects re-embed a social, ethical and political dimension? With what limits and implications? Can this open the space for emancipatory politics, or is it yet another instance of capital cooptation? Or, perhaps, even both?

With this enquiry, I want to analyse how social entrepreneurs think of social entrepreneurship, and to unpack the underlying notion of sociality, ethics and politics. In this respect, this book may be regarded as an ethnographic study on how the neoliberal subject par excellence – the entrepreneur of the self – attempts to retrieve and reclaim their political and ethical agency, and what the implications and limits of this endeavour are. To achieve this, I am seeking to deduce social entrepreneurs' regime of truth, that is, 'the types of discourse' that the social entrepreneur 'harbours and causes to function as true' (Foucault, 1977: 12–13), the kind of discourse that an individual has to hold as true to develop a social entrepreneurial subjectivity. As Foucault argues, the acceptance of a regime of truth is related to a process of subjectivation (Foucault, 2014). Therefore, the analysis of the regime of truth of social entrepreneurship includes a hermeneutic of the social entrepreneurial subject. At stake there is the question of how the aforementioned reconciliation between ethical ends and entrepreneurial means takes place at the level of the self, how it becomes thinkable and doable for social entrepreneurs. But first, we must delve into the lifeworld of the entrepreneur, familiarise ourselves with their surroundings and understand the field of action in which they seek to fashion the ethical self that will ultimately – at least they hope – make money doing good.

NOTE

1. The centrality of the production of subjectivity at work applies not only to highly skilled, managerial or the so-called creative jobs, but also in the service economy, which has been rebranded as 'experience economy'. Emma Dowling's self-ethnography of waitressing is exemplar in this respect. Drawing on her ten years' experience as a waitress, and offering thick descriptions of a period of eighteen months of full-time employment in a top-quality restaurant, Dowling shows how, in order to produce and deliver the 'dining experience', she was required to engage in affective activities – being 'enthusiastic', entertaining the customers, anticipating their desires and so forth – leveraging on her own being, that is, 'being herself' (Dowling, 2007: 120).

Chapter III

Becoming a Social Entrepreneur

One warm evening in June, I went to have a drink with Anita, an Italian woman in her early thirties. She was wearing denim overalls, red Doc Martens and a flowered cotton T-shirt. Anita was born in a small village on the border of Switzerland and had studied maths and music. She was raised by conservative parents in an upper-class environment. 'I did not share their values', she said. 'I was looking for something a bit more authentic, something that differs from the status quo'. This is why she decided to leave her parents' place at the age of eighteen (quite young for an average Italian) to move to Milan, where she studied design at Politecnico to follow her 'passion'.

After she graduated she found out about Impact Hub: 'I went to a couple of events at Impact Hub and realised that there were a lot of interesting people, who were doing very interesting things', she told me, enthused, sipping her glass of white wine. Impact Hub is an international network of coworking spaces for social entrepreneurs, in over 100 cities across the world, including Milan. They're a place where, for a fee, social entrepreneurs can work, meet, drink and plan their enterprises. 'After uni I was looking for a job, but didn't want to go for a corporate One, so I decided to become a hubber', she explained after a while, her glass almost empty. I asked why and how Impact Hub is the right place to look for a job. She replied as follows:

> Being a hubber is like building a career . . . you are in an informal environment so they can really see who you are and which skills you have. . . . Basically, you become friends, and then you may find a job, you know? Like, there was this guy working on a project and they needed a graphic designer, so he asked me, as we were already friends, and we knew we were sharing the same values. This is how I got my first job!

Anita's story is like many I heard, spending eighteen months conducting fieldwork in social entrepreneur hotspots like Impact Hub Milan. She articulates an equation between 'being a hubber' – not so much frequenting a coworking space as *being* a kind of person – and 'building a career'. In her specific case, the precondition for her first job was a friendship, a social tie that was premised on 'sharing the same values'. As the phrase 'it's not what you know, but who you know' attests, social ties have for a long time created networks of information flow and preferential treatment. But Anita's story illustrates something slightly different. Her social capital is derived not from the family she abandoned, but from her expression of a particular subjectivity: she is a hubber, and she has certain values. Impact Hub is where the right people can 'see you for who you really are'. 'Who you really are' must be expressed by you and recognised by others. This, Anita explains, is how you get a job.

In this chapter, we will delve into the lifeworld of social entrepreneurs, exploring the playful scene of organic cocktails and ping-pong tables, failures and embarrassments and heroic self-belief. We will uncover the subtle frustrations of a sociality that is at once voluntary and at the same time a compulsory condition of employment. At stake throughout is the production of subjectivity with the tools provided at a place like Impact Hub, where One has to be a certain kind of person to gain access and status (not to mention Impact Hub's monthly fee). Impact Hub emerges as not the playful coworking space it appears to be, but as a kind of social factory, where One's very self is the raw matter that must be fashioned with its material and discursive tools.

Understanding the production of subjectivity, far from naïvely investing individuals with total freedom, represents a necessary endeavour to study neoliberal governmentality beyond a perspective that sees the individual as merely manipulated and subjugated by dispositives of power. The question leading this research is how the social entrepreneurial subject is formed, in comparison and contrast with the neoliberal 'entrepreneur of the self'. Hearing from people like Anita, we will sketch a portrait of how people are attempting to draw on limited resources and flawed mechanisms to express their ethics through work, as they attempt to make of themselves a person that can make money while doing good.

A PLACE TO MEET

For people like Anita, who have fled their homes in search of making a difference, Impact Hub is a natural first port of call. Founded in 2005 by Jonathan Robinson, Etty Flanagan and Mark Hodge in a warehouse in the London borough of Islington, Impact Hub is an international network of coworking spaces dedicated to social innovators and entrepreneurs. It is for people, the website proclaims, who are 'Impact Makers', also affectionately known as 'hubbers'. Its tagline reads: 'Impact Hub is a home for people who believe that business doesn't end with profit, but can have a deep social and environmental purpose' (Impact Hub, 2019).

Impact Hub appeals to prospective clients' aspirational self-identification as much as their current business requirements, and their business model is cost to accommodate highly divergent needs. The cheapest, about £20 pm (£15 for start-ups), is a so-called virtual membership, which grants access to the mailing list and Impact Hub-Net (a social network that connects all Impact Hub members) and offers discounted prices for events and room booking; while the most expensive is the Hub Unlimited – about £475 (£395 for start-ups) and includes 24/7 use of the work space, complimentary tea and coffee, discounted rates for events and room booking and virtual membership. There is even a non-fee solution for those willing to work at Impact Hub as a volunteer host, in exchange for use of the space and facilities for a number of hours. At the time of writing, there are Impact Hubs in over 100 cities across five continents of the world, and more than 16,000 'hubbers'. The value proposition of Impact Hub is to offer people a 'place to meet' (Robinson, quoted in Bachmann, 2014). Jonathan Robinson, co-founder of Impact Hub, points this out emphatically in an interview for the Stanford Social Innovation Review: 'Everyone has ideas for making the world a better place . . . but where does One go to make them happen? . . . What if these people could come together in the same physical space and have a place to connect?' (Robinson, quoted in Bachmann, 2014). This kind of language reveals the conscious efforts to construct networks through which information can flow: ideas, experiences, advice and opportunities.

Encouragement, collaboration, exchange – these are portrayed as preconditions for changing the world, firmly situating a place like Impact Hub as a requirement for any aspiring social entrepreneur. For those with limited means for initiating or even ideating their projects, Impact Hub offers an alluring promise: turning thoughts into action, fantasy into reality. Their infrastructure for this action is a physical space where networks can be forged.

In this respect, Impact Hub offers a typical example of a coworking space. Coworking spaces can be seen as an attempt to provide a solution to the problems of independent working. Commonly conceived as shared working environments, where workers hire a desk and a Wi-Fi connection, they actually have the important function of re-socialising the work of independent workers while offering a sense of belonging. Indeed, they can be thought of as the territory where new forms of sociality that are instrumental to the organisation of work take place (Gandini, 2015; DePeuter et al., 2017; Bandinelli and Gandini, 2019). Whereas they have been portrayed as isolated, self-absorbed and detached from any form of sociality (e.g. Gurstein, 2001; Kylin and Karlsson, 2008; Kjaerulff, 2010), coworking spaces provide freelancers with tools of socialisation to sustain their careers (Wittel, 2001; Gregg, 2007; Marwick, 2013). They do so by offering what has been defined as a 'third way' of working: 'halfway between a "standard" work life within a traditional, well-delimited workplace in a community-like environment, and an independent work life as a freelancer, characteristic of freedom and independence, where the worker is based at home in isolation' (Gandini, 2015: 195). Furthermore, they offer a symbolic space, producing a narrative that functions as an identitarian dispositive (Bandinelli and Gandini, 2019). In line with this approach, Moriset defines coworking as 'serendipity accelerators designed to host creative people and entrepreneurs who endeavour to break isolation and to find a convivial environment that favours meetings and collaborations' (Moriset, 2014: 1).

This is precisely what Impact Hub promises. The idea of giving people 'a place to meet' exemplifies the extent to which Impact Hub has been thought of and designed as a place for a form of socialisation that can fulfil the twofold need of growing a sense of belonging, and maximising One's career opportunities. The opportunity for people to interact, that is, to 'come together, encourage each other, collaborate, exchange experiences and knowledge', is a promise that members will be able to produce social capital.

TOGETHER WE MAKE COMMUNITY

As within the coworking movement in general, at Impact Hub the term mostly deployed to convey this idea is 'community'. At Impact Hub Westminster (now Closed), the word 'Community' is distributed throughout the space: a sign giving instructions on how to use the kitchen facilities is entitled 'Welcome to the Community Kitchen!', and concludes by reminding hubbers that 'Together we make community'. A glass office used for meetings is decorated with big capital letters claiming 'This is community'.

As well as a motif for decorations, the concept of community is deployed to encourage – perhaps even command – a certain kind of sociality. Sociality is configured as an imperative through a regime of community and belonging that implores a certain mode of interaction between members. Assertive enough to push introverts into socialising, while open enough to be interpreted according to an individual's inclinations, 'community' serves as a discursive tool for regulating members' socialisation. This mode of socialisation is intimately connected with an aspirational vision of the self. As their tagline reads: 'We are you. We are the people you've been wanting to work with' (Impact Hub, 2016).

Questions of identity, belonging and destiny are threaded together into a biographical narrative for which the conclusion – and prize – is work. Impact Hub offers a vision of the self through working relationships and networks. This is a particularly alluring narrative for an independent worker, who has lost the company of regular colleagues and may find themselves alone in a new city, not unlike Anita. Research certainly suggests this: 48 per cent of Milanese coworkers explicitly relate to the need for a sense of community (Colleoni and Arvidsson, 2014). For entrepreneurs who find themselves alone, community is not simply a euphemism for networking opportunities, but the promise of company. Impact Hub provides social integration for entrepreneurs of the self, who find themselves detached from traditional sociocultural nets and overwhelmed by the myriad of possible biographies they could build.

There has always been a degree of sociality in the workplace. Even the office of white-collar workers in the fifties was marked by certain social structures and social practices (see, for instance, C. Wright Mills, 1956). Yet, the neoliberal redefinition of work as a means of self-actualisation has resulted in social interactions becoming a fundamental part of work. What's more, job opportunities travel through networks, and for a casualised workforce where job opportunities must be sought out on a constant basis, socialisation is necessary for survival. In short, sociality is no more just an externality, a 'desirable' part or an effect, but rather a substantial aspect of work. Making new allies becomes vital for making a living.

In this regard, it seems appropriate to remember what Carol Stone, named by newspapers as 'networking queen' and 'British best connected woman' states about friendships: 'Friends are *made*, they don't just happen, you have to work at it' (Stone, quoted in Wittel: 2001: 59, my emphasis). Stone's comments are typical of a constructionary imaginary that surrounds neoliberal sociality. Friendships are *made*; reputations are *built*. Colleoni and Arvidsson draw attention to this fact when they point to the construction of a network of contacts and the acquisition of reputation in their professional scene. Social capital is imagined as a kind of material One must accumulate and refine. It takes the form of a high-value network through which flows information (job opportunities) and preference (job offers). Rather than the theatrical imaginary that has dominated theories of sociality in the 20th century, where people are thought to learn roles and perform selves, we might better think of neoliberal sociality as a kind of construction. What One builds – the commodity of their social labour – is a network. What has to be put to work, then, is One's ability to socialise.

What single individuals buy when subscribing to Impact Hub is not so much a shared desk, or the complimentary tea and coffee, but rather discursive and material tools for producing sociality. This implies the collapse of

> of the founder, guess why? Guess who is taking over the application for the last grant? The friend of another founder.

Claudia evidences the frustration of being excluded from the networks of information and preference constructed through Impact Hub. What's more, she exposes the hierarchies inherent in networks, where some people – nodes – are better connected, exert more influence and are in control of more opportunities. Giulio replies to these sort of critiques as follows:

> The Hub has a strong brand that communicates strongly this idea of community to attract many diverse people to stimulate their creativity through the projects that take place both at a local level and within the global network, so in this sense we are open. But, from the outside, we are indeed perceived as a somewhat close community. . . . Surely, once you get into the Hub, you feel like in a family, hence if you are not 'connected', if you are not part of the club by paying at least 20 euro plus VAT, you are out indeed.

Giulio's claim is that there is a single mechanism of inclusion – the fee, which provides access to the space and facilities – to a single network: the hubbers. Claudia contests this claim: even within Impact Hub, she explains, there are further layers of access One needs to gain entry to – networks within networks. Access, Claudia told me, is premised not only on the entry fee, but on the ability to elicit connections and forge bonds once that access has been granted. For some, like Anita, the right connection will be made and lead to a job; for others, like Claudia, the right connection will not be made, and they will be left with the frustration of being excluded. Work, then, is a question not only of One's primary skill set but of making the right connections through a sociality that is, in the end, as compulsory as the 20 euro monthly fee.

SEXY SALADS AND SOCIALITY

What can be said about the sociality that must be performed in order to produce networks? One element is its ethical nature. The connection between social relationships and ethical values derives from the fact that One of the requirements for establishing relationships is to display and prove the willingness to have a 'positive impact' – in other words, to be an 'impact maker' as Impact Hub brands its members, therefore to show a virtuous character. The barriers of inclusion and exclusion from the scene revolve around the embodiment of a number of ethical principles that are thought to characterise and distinguish social entrepreneurial subjects (Bandinelli and Arvidsson, 2013).

Impact Hub's tagline reads: 'We are a network of collaborators focused on making a positive impact in our world' (Impact Hub, 2016), pointing at how the element of socialisation – being 'a network of collaborators' – is related and functional to an ethical objective 'making a positive impact in our world'. In order to successfully engage in Impact Hub sociality, the individual has to embody a certain ethos. What takes place at Impact Hub is the production of this ethos, which is effected by means of practices that I define as devices for the subjectivation of members. These are implemented in every Impact Hub across the world and constitute a core service that Impact Hub offers its members. Each of these practices can been thought of as producing an ethos based on the values of collaboration and sharing which make up the core of coworking movement narratives. To illustrate this point, I consider three examples: business clinics, 'skills-sharing' sessions and weekly lunches.

The first are workshops or free counselling sessions in which various topics related to running an enterprise (from accounting to crowdfunding) are explored. As Vera, Impact Hub manager of Milan, explained: 'we offer this service to give our community members the chance to get advice on their business plan'. 'Skill-sharing' sessions revolve around the same principle and may take different forms, but they all derive from the belief that knowledge is something to be shared, collaboratively. At Impact Hub Westminster, there used to be a project called Academy at the Hub that provides weekly classes on topics related to entrepreneurship. Their description is built on the idea of sharing as the best way of learning: 'participants are coming to sessions as much to meet other participants and share experiences as to hear from the presenter' (Impact Hub Academy, 2016). Finally, Sexy Salads are weekly lunches where everyone is encouraged to bring an ingredient to contribute to the creation of a salad. The tablemates are then encouraged to present themselves through a very short speech, in fact an elevator pitch.

Business Clinics, skill-sharing sessions and Sexy Salads can be thought of as social, material and discursive devices that combine the values of sharing and collaboration, with those of entrepreneurship. By participating to these social events, individuals are exposed to the ethos of Impact Hub. People are invited to collaborate – by offering or receiving advices, sharing their knowledge on a subject, or bringing their favourite ingredients – and at the same time they can learn the practices and dispositions that characterise the social entrepreneur. By participating in these events, individuals have the chance to embody a certain ethos by fostering a specific conduct.

Importantly, such a process of embodiment may be unsuccessful. Failures demonstrate how the production of a certain conduct is based on the development and deployment of a number of non-written norms. In this respect, I recount an episode regarding Alfredo, an Italian man in his late twenties, who at the time of the fieldwork was working as a member host at Impact

Hub Westminster, while developing an idea for his social enterprise. He once told me the story of when he brought the wrong ingredient to a Sexy Salad:

> I love the idea of Sexy Salads, and I was looking forward to participating in my first One – it's a shared meal, it's a great occasion to meet people! But I brought some Sainsbury's chicken. I thought it was ok, I mean . . . I eat chicken . . . but the others were almost disgusted, you should have seen their faces. They said it politely, in the British way, but I could tell they felt almost offended. . . . Well . . . I apologised and left. . . . I guess I've learnt you cannot bring meat to a Sexy Salad. . . . I think next week I'll bring some pumpkin seeds or quinoa.

This anecdote demonstrates that the invitation to 'share' and collaborate in a common project, in this case a Sexy Salad, is subjected to non-written rules. Alfredo broke One of these and therefore was not welcome, but instead judged quite severely. Such a mistake, a misunderstanding of what the principles of sharing include and exclude in the context of Impact Hub, caused him to lose the opportunity to socialise, as he could not get the opportunity he was looking forward to: that is, 'to meet people'. If, as Goodenough put it, a culture 'consists of whatever it is One has to know or believe in order to operate in a manner acceptable to its members' (quoted in Geertz, 1973: 5), then Impact Hub's culture requires the knowledge and enactment of certain ethical principles, be they expressed through events or gastronomically. These ethical principles serve as a kind of language, in which hubbers must be fluent in order to see a return on their social labour. Sexy Salads exemplify the way that a variety of objects can be enlisted as One of Impact Hub's discursive tools for producing sociality.

DO YOU MEAN A POP-UP THINK TANK?

A further example of the inherent code of conduct of sociality at Impact Hub regards the deployment of a certain lexicon. Using a particular vocabulary is essential to attracting the attention of fellow hubbers, and therefore to socialising with them. During the first weeks of my fieldwork, when I was making the first attempts to get to know hubbers, I soon realised my language was a barrier. Deploying an academic discourse, One that focuses on formulating questions and critique of a current state of affairs, was ineffective. To attract hubbers' attention, I had to rethink the way in which to present my project. I decided to suggest that a few hubbers organise a seminar in which they would have the opportunity to voice their view about social entrepreneurship so as to arrive at a shared definition. The collaborative character of the seminar, and the formulation of a common objective seemed to be more akin to the ethos of hubbers. The substance of the activities had not varied that much; in the end, I wanted to get the chance to ask social entrepreneurs their opinion on social entrepreneurship, its ethical and political character, yet I used a different language. I myself had to engage in a form of sociality with a specialised language, perform a subjectivity that was compatible with their ethos to gain access to my own opportunities. Below is an excerpt from my fieldwork notes recounting this attempt:

> Today I got the opportunity to approach Alfredo and Sophia in the Hub kitchenette. I have already engaged in a few discussions with Alfredo, and I know he is working on a project with Sophia, a French woman working part time for an IT corporation and using her spare time to 'understand more about social entrepreneurship'. I greeted them, smiled, and asked them how their projects were going. I knew Alfredo was in the idea generation phase of his start-up. Alfredo told me he had had a meeting with a famous social entrepreneur and that he had agreed to be an SEI ambassador. I did not fully understand what this meant, but refrained from asking further questions. Sophia said she was organising a workshop on community development. She invited me to join and I said that I would. Then I told them about my idea of 'organising a seminar' for social entrepreneurs to discuss their ideas on the politics and ethics of social entrepreneurship, and pointed out that 'to have a coherent idea of the political function of social entrepreneurship could be vital for the strength of the movement'. Alfredo stayed silent for a bit. Sophia continued preparing her organic filtered coffee. Then Alfredo said 'Do you mean something like a pop-up think tank?'

In the end, we never organised either a seminar, or a pop-up think tank. But this episode demonstrates well how the use of certain jargon, which reflects a modality of thinking, a value horizon, is central to the sociality of social entrepreneurs. Failure to deploy a given terminology, and to frame ideas and projects in a certain way, impedes the process of socialisation from taking place; to use hubbers' vocabulary, it prevents friends from being made, and therefore jeopardises the opportunity to find new work. These vignettes reveal that Impact Hub is a place where ethically burdened socialisation is produced. What Alfredo broke, indeed, was an ethical rule: to shop in a big supermarket and to eat meat is considered wrong. What I failed to do was deploy a certain language; to express, by means of words, a series of specific values. The ability of the individual to establish relationships, those relationships that are a necessary condition for her to advance in her career, is subjected to the ability to learn and enact a certain ethos.

What I want to flag up here is that to engage in a process of socialisation at Impact Hub One has to learn and deploy a certain ethos that reproduces a certain set of values and beliefs, a certain regime of truth. For example, One has to learn what can be shared or not shared, what can be consumed, where to shop and what language to use when expressing ideas. Impact Hub sociality is produced based on these norms, and Impact Hub is the place where these norms, this code of conduct, are produced and reproduced. To use Foucauldian parlance: Impact Hub is an *ethopoios* for it 'possesses the quality of transforming ethos' (Foucault, 2005: 237).

HEROIC SELF-CONFIDENCE[1]

Sergio, who we encountered earlier, confided in me that he has always had self-confidence issues. 'I could never fully test myself, I was too scared of failure', he admitted during One of our first conversations. Eventually, he started working full time for a social cooperative that is One of the most influential actors in the Italian social entrepreneurship network. Sergio immediately recognised the ethical burden of sociality and used to feel deeply uncomfortable about it: 'All this buzz about changing the world etc.', he told me, with the tone of One who is talking about something so ephemeral and impossible that does not even require further clarification: 'They really wanted me to buy into it', he continued 'but I couldn't fully believe in this story'. At the time, he was motivated by a different set of reasons: 'I was working there cause I needed the money, and okay, it was better to work for some good guys than for the corporate sharks, but still. . . . I just did not feel like I was changing the world or anything like that, I did not feel part of them. And this made me suffer, I felt excluded'.

Sergio's story demonstrates how the embodiment of an ethos is necessary to do One's job. To work in a given field he had to foster an ethos, to promote and communicate a set of values to which he wasn't naturally inclined. And I can sympathise with him: to believe that you can change the world, and to make substantial sacrifices on the basis of that belief, requires enormous self-confidence. Much of the discourse that surrounds social entrepreneurship reflects the need for this kind of confidence and self-belief. The mythic narratives we encountered in chapter II, where the social entrepreneur is conceived as a kind of messianic hero, is a discursive device that not only regulates social entrepreneurs' behaviour through instilling an ethical ethos, but a tool that they can use to work on themselves, to reconfigure their patterns of thought, and produce a subjectivity that can muster the confidence on which social entrepreneurship depends. This is precisely what Sergio describes happened to him. For Sergio, frequenting Impact Hub resulted in a change in his approach towards his career, and therefore in his mode of thinking about himself and his future. Before being a Hubber, he thought differently about his opportunities and what was possible. Engaging with Impact Hub sociality, he developed a specific subjectivity, fashioned himself in a certain way and generated a form of social capital derived from self-belief.

This case highlights the productive nature of Impact Hub's sociality. What is produced is a certain kind of self. An ethical endeavour is involved: a process by which One makes himself or herself a certain subject and that includes our response to invitations or injunctions to make oneself into a certain kind of person. Social entrepreneurs' sociality at Impact Hub involves a process of self-fashioning that is essential for them to enter the scene and, eventually, the market.

After a few months, Sergio told me, 'Now I can say I am a hubber, as I think like a hubber, but also I must admit that I had to become One, I had to believe certain things if I wanted to expand my portfolio!' Sergio's reflections highlight the inherent connection between the compulsory, opportunistic, and ethical character of social entrepreneurs' sociality at Impact Hub, and how they cooperate to produce certain kinds of people. To put this connection in a schematic way: individuals subscribe to Impact Hub to meet other people who can offer them career opportunities by means of partnerships or collaborations; to get these opportunities One has to establish relationships with other individuals, therefore to engage in a process of socialisation; this process is regulated by a set of values and can effectively take place only if One learns and embodies a certain ethos; this process of learning and embodiment is a process of subjectivation. Following this, coworking spaces can be interpreted as devices for the production of a subjectivity that is instrumental to work. In this respect, they articulate a formalisation of the process of the investment of the self that is peculiar to entrepreneurialised individuals in neoliberal economies.

Impact Hub's function, or rather its value proposition, is to offer the opportunity to develop an ethos via engaging and learning a modality of socialisation that is mandatory for furthering a career project in the scene of social entrepreneurship. In other words, being a hubber entails and demands the development of a certain subjectivity, which is instrumental in entering the job market, and unfolds in a specific form of sociality.

FAKE IT TILL YOU MAKE IT

The discourses that produce and glorify the ideal-type of the social entrepreneur can be experienced as rather patronising. Karina, a Polish woman in her mid-twenties with a background in social work and studying for an MA in social entrepreneurship, recounted the negative effect that a supposedly 'inspirational' guest lecture had on her:

> There was this speaker, One who wrote a very famous book on how to be a successful social entrepreneur, I don't remember the title now. . . . Well, he was

> saying a lot about how you should be, like you should be brave, and take risk, and be confident, and brand yourself. . . . But I felt so bad! Because I am rather shy, and don't know if I am brave enough, and I kind of hate self-branding.

Saanvi, an Indian woman in her late twenties, was One of Karina's classmates. Before coming to London, she worked in India for a non-governmental organisation (NGO) supporting victims of forced marriage. I met her at Impact Hub Westminster, where she was doing an internship as part of her degree. Her feelings were similar to those of Karina. She told me that 'all this talk about how social entrepreneurs should be is just so annoying. They make me doubt myself in a way that is discouraging. . . . Can I just be who I am? Or do I have to become someone else to be a social entrepreneur?'.

The experiences of Karina and Saanvi evidence that a supposedly inspirational narrative can be perceived as discouraging and annoying. To be sure, different individuals negotiate with the discourses of social entrepreneurship in different ways, and may well challenge or refuse them. Yet, both Karina and Saanvi recognised the importance of developing a certain attitude in order to be taken seriously as potential entrepreneurs. This is what Karina said in a subsequent interview:

> I don't know if I am the right person to be a social entrepreneur, but if there is something that I learnt during this MA it is that, at least, I must to pretend. And now I have started to. . . . Like I go to people and say, 'I am a social entrepreneur, I am working on this project etc'. And in a way, it is working, like the more you say these things the more you end up believing in them.

Saavi remarked:

> After all, what they are teaching us is how to turn what we like and want to do in a business plan, which is not very easy, but I guess is what One needs to do to clarify her ideas, and also to convince other people of the value of these ideas.

These examples are indicative of the fact that a guided process of adaptation of the self to the form of the enterprise is part of the education of social entrepreneurs aspirants. This is supposed to bring the individual towards the identification with an ideal 'social entrepreneur'. This might be questioned by social entrepreneurs aspirants, but they tend to recognise its strategic value, and the potential benefits in terms of self-confidence and credibility.

WORKING ON THE SELF

Working on the self has been One of the pillars of westernised modern and postmodern culture, which – highly influenced by the psychoanalytic vulgate (Illouz, 2007) – has posed self-scrutiny, interpretation and construction as inevitable and desirable practices. The conception of the self shifted from 'something given' to something that must be created, from an object of discovery to an object of craft. This process of self-fashioning is One defining trait of entrepreneurial subjects in general and social entrepreneurs in particular.

As Wittel (2001) has observed, at stake is a commodification of relationships, as they are made into material to be exchanged. This gets deeply merged with a 'playful' conduct, context and atmosphere, for the majority of networking events involve leisure activities such as consuming alcohol or listening to music. Networking, remarks Wittel, is also deeply related to individualisation, for it is the very personality of the individual, their charisma, their social capital, that must be effectively expressed to be a successful networker. As Virno pinpoints, at stake there is an opportunistic 'emotional tonality' (Virno, 2003) that makes the individual very strategic in choosing how to invest time: valuable contacts, that is, those who can get to a new job or partnership, are obviously preferred, and time is rarely dedicated to interactions that do not add value to One's career.

A prominent trait of social entrepreneurs is the high investment of their selves in their professional activities. In what has been named 'dis-organised capitalism', where individuals work outside of institutions, social entrepreneurs have to 'do the work of the structures by themselves' (McRobbie, 2002: 158). Social entrepreneurs, especially when they are the founders of One-person enterprises (as is often the case in the first phases of start-ups), represent this very structure in a precise way. Notably, the reflexive narrative of social entrepreneurship draws heavily on the idea that the enterprise must emerge spontaneously from the self. But in reality, as we saw with Sergio, there is very little spontaneity involved. Instead, it is highly wrought and contrived, much like the 'accelerated serendipity' of coworking spaces' sociality. Things that we might think of as natural inclinations – who we socialise with, what kind of outlook we have – are reconfigured as material to be refined, honed and perfected in order to become a social entrepreneur. And what might thought of voluntary is, in fact, work that is a tacit condition of employment. The tools for this work are rented by Impact Hub, which functions as a factory for the production of sociality and subjectivities.

CONCLUSION

The argument outlined in this chapter is that Impact Hub's forms of sociality entail a process of subjectivation that is essential and instrumental to One's career. In other words, the production of subjectivity is the condition of existence of a social status that, in turn, is vital to gain a valuable market position. I have built this argument through a series of steps: firstly, we have seen that sociality lies at the core of the coworking movement and that it is the main reason for individuals subscribing to Impact Hub. Secondly, we have interpreted this sociality as compulsory and opportunistic – for individuals at Impact Hub must produce and engage in specific forms of sociality in order to build their career – and as characterised by a series of technologies that allows individuals to learn a code of conduct, an ethos. Thirdly, we have seen that the process of learning how to engage in Impact Hub's compulsory and opportunistic sociality can be thought of as a process of subjectivation through which individuals develop an ethos that is ultimately instrumental to surviving in the job market.

This socialisation's process, origin and objective can be described as follows: (i) One has to meet potential work partners or employers; (ii) One has to establish relationships of mutual affection on the basis of a supposedly authentic disclosure of the self with these potential partners; (iii) to do that One has to perform and embody a specific ethos. This process indicates a combination of a functional type of socialisation with an ethical nature. The function of coworking spaces in general, and Impact Hub in particular, is to provide the discursive and material forms of organisation for these elements to profitably combine. Indeed, going to Impact Hub, individuals engage in a sociality that leads them to accumulate ethical and social capital, which on their turn are functional to capture market opportunities. This sociality can be seen as a form of work organisation. This resonates with the network sociality described by Wittel (2001) and of course does not escape the exploitative dynamic described by critical theorists and cultural scholars. Yet, it shows the unprecedented prominence of an ethical stance. Indeed, while the production of subjectivity and identity has always been at the core of work in neoliberal societies, for social entrepreneurs, this seems to have become a very much organised and formalised process.

This ethically charged sociality reflects the paradoxical feature of social entrepreneurship, for it is built upon a combination of individualistic and ethical elements (Bandinelli and Gandini, 2019). But what are these ethical elements, and what is the regime of truth that individuals accept when engaging in a process of subjectivation as social entrepreneurs? How does this subject combine ethical values with inherent individualism? This is the topic of next chapter.

NOTES

1. An extended version of the story of Sergio has been published in Bandinelli, C. (2019). The production of subjectivity in neoliberal culture industries: the case of coworking spaces. International Journal of Cultural Studies. https://doi.org/10.1177/1367877919878449

Chapter IV

The Good, the Bad and the Millennials

The Ethical Inward Turn

Ethics is traditionally understood as the study of the One's behaviour towards others. How should we treat other people? How do we deserve to be treated by them? In social entrepreneurship, we encounter something different. For the social entrepreneur, who abandons a life of relative comfort for the risks of an enterprise, ethics is understood as a need for self-expression – to enact One's true identity. This is not to say that social entrepreneurs do not seek to help others and succeed in doing so, but that their ethical behaviour is conceived as an inherent feature of their identity that must be expressed. Ethics first emerges from the needs of the individual, rather than the needs of others.

In this chapter, we will explore this ethical inward turn, where ethics is understood as an irresistible need for self-expression. While it might be tempting to discard social entrepreneurs' ethics as self-serving – the conversion of an ethical responsibility towards others into a form of self-attendance – this chapter considers social entrepreneurs' ethics within the context of conflictual demands placed upon the contemporary early-career subject. This subject is heir to a politically hyper-aware culture, One that expects them to be versant in a range of political issues and cognizant of the flaws and injuries of capitalism. At the same time, they are expected to be able to consume and signify wealth during an economic downturn. How are they to reconcile the competing demands of being, as it were, woke and rich? Such a problem, posed in such a way, leaves the subject destined to fail as an individual.

This chapter is interested in social entrepreneur's resolution to this problem: how to accumulate both financial and ethical capital even where the two come into conflict. We will see how this search for resolution is driven by what is often experienced as an unbearable personal malaise. As we proceed, we may consider this malaise as a peculiarly contemporary condition, whereby the neoliberal injunction to actualise One's identity through work has coerced the contemporary subject to express all ethical inclinations through a career and as part of a solitary appraisal of what constitutes good and bad. This implies that the self has to be interrogated, consulted, with the enterprise ideally emerging out of a process of self-enquiry. Through this process, individual solutions are sought to systemic problems: in the absence of a collective conception of ethics, political problems are answered by individuals.

ETHICAL INWARD TURN

On 8th of November 2011, I began my first day as a host at Impact Hub Westminster. One of the first people I met was Alfredo. Alfredo was in his late twenties and had moved to London to study an MA in international management at Imperial College. When he finished the MA, he decided to dedicate all his time to founding a social enterprise, named SEI. On that afternoon, we had a long conversation. I was keen on exploring the chain of events that led him to leave his (and incidentally also my) country to come to London and try to become a social entrepreneur. Alfredo was willing to talk. He told me that in Italy, before leaving, he was working for a big corporation, earning quite a lot of money. But he couldn't continue: the routine of a job didn't reflect his values, and this was damaging his mental health:

> I had an MA in Economics, and was working for American Express, earning a high salary. I also had a girlfriend of six years, we were in love, I guess. Plus, of course, there was my family. On the surface my life was just perfect. But I was depressed. Really depressed. Because the job I was doing . . . I didn't care about the money and the security and all those things. . . . I was so down I needed to take drugs as I couldn't bear to think of living all my life doing things that go against my values, just forgetting who I am . . . I wanted to change things! I wanted to improve other people's lives!

Alfredo could probably have lived a more comfortable life in his native city, with a high salary and a stable relationship. Yet, he felt an intolerable discomfort in seeing himself as someone who was not doing anything for others, that is, 'changing things'. He wanted to take on an active role in the quest to improve the circumstances in which humanity lives, and he renounced financial and – to an extent – emotional comfort, to pursue this objective. When I met him, he was earning no money at all, investing all his savings in the dream of becoming a social entrepreneur and changing 'how things are'. What is evident in his words is how ethical motives come to prominence and outweigh financial Ones.

Noemi, a thirty-year-old woman form Sardinia running a social enterprise dedicated to urban regeneration projects, had a similar story. 'I had been working for a consultancy company for 5 years. I earned quite a lot. So, financially speaking, nothing to complain about', she told me, sipping her glass of prosecco. 'But I was not doing anything I really believed in, I was not being myself. . . . Eventually I just gave up and started this social enterprise project . . . I started a year ago and haven't earned a cent yet . . . zero'. I ventured an apparently simple question: 'Why are you doing it then?' She replied with an equally simple answer: 'Well . . . I might sound naïve, but I am doing it because I want to change the world!'

'I was the CEO of a major bank', Sara, another aspiring social entrepreneur in Italy, told me. Sara, an Italian woman in her mid-thirties, came from a disadvantaged area in the south of the country. She talks about her life as divided into two: before and after becoming a social entrepreneur. I interviewed her during lunch in an organic restaurant in central London. This is how she began talking about her journey towards social entrepreneurship: 'as you can imagine, money was not a problem. . . . But, you know, I was not doing anything to improve the world, anything which corresponded to my ideals. . . . This was just not good for me'. I asked her why: 'I wanted to do something to innovate! To change people's behaviour!' she said. Following this feeling, she decided to quit her job, and after volunteering for a few months in Asia, came back home to set up a social enterprise that offers work to female prisoners and produces shopping bags from recycled fabric wastes. What I want to highlight here is Sara's focus upon herself. Her enterprise emerged not from an appraisal of female prisoners, but rather from her appraisal of what 'was just not good' for her. The good, here, is firmly rooted in Sara's own self; it is from self-appraisal that she derives the passion to help others.

Alfredo, Noemi and Sara's stories illustrate what I am calling an ethical inward turn. Their ethical motivations emerge from attending to the self, to their own existential needs. Ethics is therefore acted out at the place of the personal, becoming a question of actualising individual qualities and aspirations perceived as authentically emerging from the self. I am therefore using the term 'ethical inward turn' not to emphasise a self-centredness of Alfredo, Noemi and Sara's ethics, but to illustrate that their ethical action emerges from looking inwards rather than outwards. This inward turn constituted of several key features which I will go on to explore in more detail: (i) self-discovery, experienced as emotional suffering transformed into ethical action; (ii) self-improvement through the ethical enterprise, which I interpret in terms of Foucault's ethical concept of 'the care of the self'; (iii) the subsequent resignification of wealth, where financial capital is depreciated in value in relation to ethical action such that expensive objects are rendered irrelevant or in bad taste; and (iv) an individualisation, where ethics derives from personal circumstances, characteristics and judgements rather than collectively agreed objectives and principles. In the remainder of this chapter, we will explore each of these phases of the social entrepreneurial ethical narrative, and their implications for social entrepreneurship's model of ethics.

SELF-DISCOVERY

Alfredo, Noemi and Sara's stories all hinge on an epiphanic moment of self-discovery. This self-discovery, which initiates the individual on the road to social entrepreneurship, tends to emerge out of a state of personal malaise or suffering. Alfredo describes the thought of not helping others 'unbearable'. His life in the comfortable, but ethically empty, corporate world caused what he described as a deep depression. Ethics is here understood as both an obligation to others and to the self, a visceral need that, typically, corporate life has denied them. Sara explains that her inability to express her ethical desires 'was just not good for me', similarly configuring ethics in terms of its negative impact upon oneself rather than others. Ethical discourses and actions become a matter of projecting One's own personal values, desires and beliefs.

The failure to do that results in individual emotional conditions – depression, dissatisfaction – rather than in a moral sense of inadequacy, or in suffering for the circumstances of the others to whom One has failed to respond. 'I was depressed', claims Alfredo; 'that was just not good for me' remarks Sara; 'I was not being myself', says Noemi. Making money was insufficient when it wasn't accompanied by doing good. This realisation takes a form of self-discovery, akin to a religious epiphany that sets the hero on a new path.

'I am investing everything I have, I am not doing anything else. After all, you cannot change the world part time!' Alfredo exclaimed to me, depicting himself both as a foolish contemporary hero, and as a very serious person, someone who works full time. Ethical action is narrated as a vocation, or even a calling. Enea, a London-based Italian man in his mid-thirties, expressed precisely this sentiment. After completing an MA in Environmental Design, he started volunteering for charities and associations, mainly in the field of waste collections and upcycling. During this time, he could afford working for free because of a good sum of money he inherited in his early twenties. After a couple of years, he started feeling lost, and in need to find a proper job. He wanted to feel he was 'useful to society'. Then, he enrolled to an MA in social entrepreneurship to 'learn how to find a job that can allow to have an impact'. His story follows precisely the same narrative of personal malaise leading to self-discovery, the response to which is social entrepreneurship. During an informal interview in a 'maker-space' in Peckham, south-east London, he told me: 'I have now found my motivation. If by means of work I can do positive things, then I am willing to work, to build a career. It's like a calling for me!'

Alfredo and Enea's accounts illustrate a need to express an ethical calling that cannot be fulfilled by part time volunteering or ethical action within One's informal social world. Instead, it must be expressed and implemented through work. Work, or more specifically the enterprise, provides both the instrument of ethical action and the accreditation of 'actually' doing something rather than simply signifying ethical aspirations. The epiphanic moment of self-discovery, which must be significant enough to compel the individual to subvert the material basis of their lives (job, city, relationship, etc.), is what initiates the subject on the journey towards the social enterprise. Self-discovery creates the question – how can I express my ethical values? – that the social enterprise answers.

SELF-IMPROVEMENT AND SELF-MANAGEMENT

Once initiated on this path, the aspiring social entrepreneur must actively work on themselves in order to hone the self that they have provisionally discovered. Working on the self is a necessary step for any career in which the very features of the self are considered as a form of capital to be invested. Social entrepreneurs are confronted with a range of discursive tools that they can (or must) use to nurture their ethical inclinations into a useable subjectivity in the professional field.

Whether One enrols for an MA in social entrepreneurship, or makes enquiries to an important association in the field, or just buys a how-to book, One will be faced with a series of more or less explicit questions that are designed to explain what it means to be a social entrepreneur and how to start this way of life, this mode of being. Generally, these questions are modelled on topics such as 'how it feels' to be a social entrepreneur, what social entrepreneurs think, which kind of life they want to live. Social entrepreneurs aspirants are led through a process of self-consultation, in order to discover whether they have the right attitude, values and drives to fulfil the expectations of social entrepreneurship.

Unlimited (Unltd), a UK-based association funded 2002, whose declared objective is to 'create a future where enterprising people are transforming our world for good' (Unltd, 2019), released a free toolkit that is designed to give guidance to social entrepreneurs aspirants. The first chapter is dedicated to taking them through a sort of quality-check of their reasons for seeking change. It is not enough to want to 'avoid a corporate job' or to 'become rich', or to 'change the world', it is essential to be totally clear about One's objectives and the way to achieve them:

> Starting an enterprise requires that you need to decide for yourself what you want to achieve, what you consider to be a success and what it is you hope to

> achieve in the short as well as the long term. This applies to both you and the enterprise that you are thinking of starting.
>
> (Unltd, 2016a)

While this is true of entrepreneurship in general, it is even more important for social entrepreneurs, as they face an even harder challenge:

> As a social entrepreneur, you will be expected to generate profits, prove that you are creating measurable positive change and improving the planet, or at least not damaging it – otherwise known as the 3 P's: Profit, Planet and People.
>
> (Unltd, 2016a: 3)

By means of this prescriptive advice, social entrepreneurs aspirants are encouraged to examine their objectives and to assess them in relation to the expectations of making profit and 'improving the planet'. These two goals, whose coupling defines social entrepreneurship as such, imply the need to develop an entrepreneurial personality and then to deploy this in order to solve social problems.

'How-to' books on business modelling adopt an analogous pedagogical approach. The best seller *Business Model Generation*, in full sight in Impact Hub Westminster's library, begins with a set of questions that lead through a process of self-assessment. Again, before embarking on the journey of business modelling, One should make sure he or she possesses the right personality:

Are you an entrepreneurial spirit?
Yes ___ No___
Are you constantly thinking about how to create values and build new businesses, or how to improve or transform your organisation?
Yes ___ No___
Are you trying to find innovative ways to do business to replace old, outdated Ones?
Yes ___ No___

(Osterwalder and Pigneur, 2009: 7)

These questions are of the kind that imply and impose the right answer, being so general that it is almost impossible to answer in the affirmative to at least One question. Accordingly, the following page reads: 'If you have answered "yes" to any of these questions, welcome to our group!' (Osterwalder and Pigneur, 2009: 8). Social entrepreneurs aspirants will find that they are 'entrepreneurial spirits', hence entitled to be welcomed to the 'group' – a group that is supposedly populated by 'visionaries, gamechangers and challengers'

(Osterwalder and Pigneur, 2009: 8), terms mobilised as highly desirable. One is both born a social entrepreneur, and must work to become One.

Academic discourses may replicate this pattern. As part of my preliminary fieldwork, I attended the first lessons of the Entrepreneurial Business Modelling module for a postgraduate course in social entrepreneurship at a well-known University college in London. The course convenor opened the lecture stating that: 'First of all, you have to understand why you are the right person to run a business'. For that purpose, students were asked a set of pivotal questions, such as:

> What sort of environment do you want to work in?
> What sort of skills do you have?
> What sort of skills do you need to improve?
> What are your values?
> How do you want me to see you?
> What is your ambition?

What is involved is the production, which has to be felt of as a discovery, of the entrepreneurial self. These methods are meant to reveal which parts of the self can be successfully actualised, objectified, into the ethos of the archetypical social entrepreneur, an activity in which the subject has to engage in order to discover the 'entrepreneurial self'. This discovery is actually a hermeneutical production: the subject has to shape itself, activating the right aspects of character. The plethora of 'how-to' books on social entrepreneurship offer a vast number of recipes on how to forge, test and check One's personality.

Reading these books, social entrepreneurs aspirants acknowledge they should be: 'innovative, resourceful, practical and opportunistic', motivated not only by achieving the 'deal' but also the 'ideal' (Elkington, 2008: 3). Also, they are expected to be 'very serious about learning from, and applying business experience and ideas to social questions. . . . Fundamentally interested in what works in practice and how you scale up ideas to achieve effective growth. . . . Very focused' (Mawson, 2008: 7). Furthermore, they would have to think of themselves as considering 'the world differently' and seeing 'opportunities where others see challenges' (Ashton, 2010: 4). In other words, they have to be able to 'transform their dreams into fledgling programmes' (Boschee, 2006: 356).

While the discursive tools for self-improvement recall the self-help literature of personal growth with the intentionally ambiguous imagery of horoscopes, there is a more significant theoretical thread running through its attempts to help the reader make of themselves a social entrepreneur. This thread can be best described in terms of Foucault's concept of the care of the self. In the last years of his life and research, Michel Foucault closely explored the means, ends, and significance of the process through which individuals create themselves as subjects, tracing the origin of this process back to the ancient Greek notion and practices of *epimeleia heautou*, the care of the self (Foucault, 2005). As he stated in a 1983 interview, this intellectual endeavour can be thought of as a 'genealogy of ethics' (Foucault, 2000: 266) where the term 'ethics' refers to 'the kind of relationship you ought to be with yourself, *rapport a sòi*' (Foucault, 2000: 263). Therefore, ethics – regardless of the particular moral systems that may originate from it in different historical contexts – is a form of continual work on the self, a perennial activity of 'self bricolage' (Rabinow, 2000: xxxix).

There is a clear resonance between self-care and care of the self within the social entrepreneurship, which tends to originate from a situation of personal dissatisfaction or even depression. Here, ethical fulfilment has a therapeutic element, with the how-to books presenting an interweaving of personal, professional and ethical guidance. However, at the heart is an attempt to work upon One's own character in order to enact an ethical life. Rather than a perversely self-centred ethics, social entrepreneurs' inward turn is a result of work on the self.

REDEFINING PROFIT

Within the ethical paradigm of social entrepreneurship, wealth must be reconfigured in order that the twin imperatives of making money doing good are accorded their appropriate status. Most often, this involves a depreciation of value in financial wealth. Whether or not we dispute the authenticity or validity of individuals' ethical call, it at the very least signals a desire to forgo personal wealth to act in the interests of others. Virtually every social entrepreneur I met mobilised a narrative whereby financial security is abandoned to follow ethical drives. Becoming a social entrepreneur is described as primarily an ethical choice, a choice that is done in the belief of 'doing good' not only for oneself, but also for other people, even for the whole 'world', in the most emphatic cases.

Sara captures this resignification of wealth in an anecdote about her pearl:

> You know . . . since I have become a social entrepreneur I have earned no salary, and I have invested almost all the money that I had . . . but I don't mind, I quite like not having much money. . . . Before, in my previous life – cos yes, I have had two lives! – I was going to parties, wearing my pearl necklace, and now when I go to see those friends from my 'previous life' they are like: where are

> your pearls? Well . . . you know . . . I just forget to wear them! I feel I am doing something good for the world, who cares about pearls?

Sara's describes her journey into social entrepreneurship as a kind of rebirth – her 'two lives' – and this new life if marked by the depreciation in the pearls' value. The pearls' depreciation exemplifies the way that financial wealth is resignified as inferior or irrelevant in the light of ethical action. Sara preferred the ethical burden of social responsibility to expensive objects. Material satisfaction is here represented as ephemeral in comparison with the gratification of 'doing something for the world'.

What emerges from the words of Alfredo, Sara and Noemi is that ethical motivations are ascribed a primary role in shaping One's working life, to the point that they outweigh the importance of personal profit. Indeed, virtually every social entrepreneur I met mobilised a narrative whereby financial security is abandoned to follow ethical drives. 'I had a paid job, so what?' said Alfredo; 'I quite like not having much money', echoes Sara; 'I am not doing it to earn money', declares Noemi. Such claims indicate that ethical reward is generally preferred over financial security and individual wealth, which are considered insufficient. Becoming a social entrepreneur is described as primarily an ethical choice, a choice that is done in the belief of 'doing good' not only for oneself, but also for other people, even for the whole 'world', in the most emphatic cases. For Alfredo, to 'not be contributing in any way to society' was 'unbearable', and Naomi happily accepted earning no salary in exchange for the pursuit of 'changing the world'.

Although these are quite vague and hyperbolic expressions, they signal the presence of an ethical ambition and articulate an ethical discourse that exceeds the private dimension of individual profit. To 'change the world' may mean many different things, but it surely indicates the attempt to care for the other than itself. In this respect, the narratives deployed by social entrepreneurs revolve around responsiveness towards the other, and are indicative of the will to turn entrepreneurship into an ethical practice, that is, a practice aimed at maximising collective happiness. To this extent, social entrepreneurs challenge the notion of the narrowly self-interested entrepreneur of the self, who is structurally incapable of social solidarity and responsibility. On the other hand, redefining profit entails reconfiguring the relative value of what we might think of as social entrepreneurship's double profit: financial and ethical capital.

What social entrepreneurs challenge is exactly the idea that engaging in entrepreneurial activities is inherently incompatible with an ethical vocation. For this statement to be embraced, entrepreneurial means and profit have to be redefined as ethically neutral. As long as the latter is perceived as the result of competitive and individualised conduct, something like a social enterprise remains unthinkable. Social entrepreneurs are well aware of that. Indeed, the redefinition of profit is One of the distinguishing traits of the social entrepreneurship scene.

During a roundtable organised by Alfredo, I had the chance to ask a few questions about the role and notion of profit in social entrepreneurship to Amber, the CEO of One of the largest UK networks of social enterprises. Amber is a British woman in her forties. Her hair well groomed, she wore a blue suit and a white silk shirt. She had a classic fashion style, well suited to her position of power. On that occasion she declared that:

> One of the most difficult things to change is people's vision of profit, they tend to think that if you make profits then you cannot make good. But things work the opposite way . . . yesterday, at a conference, I met a lovely lady from a quite well-known social enterprise, she took it over last year and it was broke, but she is still giving money every year to charities so as to increase the impact . . . so it was a mess, she went bankrupt, she fired everybody, she stopped funding the charity etc. . . . so basically now she has no impact whatsoever. Had she made it profitable she would have still been doing good things . . . if you don't get financial things sorted you cannot get the good things sorted . . . people should be out and proud to be profitable!

Amber's discourse unfolds around two main points: the recognition of a certain common sense that sees 'profit' as antithetical to 'good', and the will to radically transform this belief. Profit, Amber explains, is essential for 'doing good', it is what makes it possible. Cristina, a social entrepreneur from Argentina who participated in the same round table, expressed a very similar view: 'The more the profit, the more the social! I don't understand why it is so difficult to get . . . where does this difficulty come from? It's business with a social aim, that's all it is', she said with the slightly annoyed tone of someone who is obliged to keep stating the obvious.

Within social entrepreneurship, profit is redefined as instrumental to ethics, as what enables ethical actions to be taken. The ethical opposition between a profit-making activity and an action directed towards the achievement of the common good is suppressed by the social entrepreneurship regime of truth through the definition of entrepreneurial tools as instruments to be possibly applied to a variety of objectives. Cristina made this point clear when, during the round table, she claimed that 'the fact that contemporary capitalism has used entrepreneurship in a way that has exacerbated social inequalities does not mean that entrepreneurship is bad, it means that it has been badly intended and used so far'. Alfredo agreed: 'Profit is nothing but One of the rewards that a person may have when solving a problem'. A similar opinion was expressed by Paul, a lecturer in social entrepreneurship who I met at the Marmelade (the fringe festival of the Skoll World Forum on social entrepreneurship). While we were having a beer in a pub, I asked him how he would define a social entrepreneur. He replied as follows: 'Entrepreneurship can be good or bad depending on the entrepreneur. A social entrepreneur will make social things with entrepreneurial tools!'

These excerpts make the point clear: entrepreneurial tools are thought of as neutral *in sé*, therefore as mere instruments with no ethical agency: they can be 'good or bad', or 'badly intended', they can be used to make good or they can be used maliciously. In this perspective, they are constructed just as enablers. What is enabled, what gets realised, are the needs, values and desires of individual entrepreneurs. For an enterprise to be social, then, it has to be the dispositive through which virtuous individuals express their ethical desires. The alleged ethical neutrality of entrepreneurial means and the private nature of ethical actions are closely related and together form the two pillars of the social entrepreneurship regime of truth. Indeed, it is only by postulating the ethical neutrality of entrepreneurship that this can be thought of as the ideal actualiser of all the possible ranges of an individual's values and virtues. Analogously, it is only by thinking of ethical actions as descending from individual's values and virtues that the autonomous and extra-institutional character of entrepreneurship can be conceived of as functional for the realisation of ethical ideals.

Such assumptions cannot be taken for granted. An evident issue concerns the nature and agency of entrepreneurial means, and leads to the question: What happens when virtues have to be translated into business plans? The complexity of such a process of translation is often removed by social entrepreneurship discourses, but it actually represents an essential critical juncture that concerns the question of the agency of entrepreneurial tools: what kinds of actions are made possible by entrepreneurial tools, and what are suppressed. In other words, what is involved is the investigation of the agency of the enterprise. This is the central topic of the next and last chapter.

THE INDIVIDUALISATION OF ETHICS

The discourses mobilised by Alfredo, Sara, Noemi and others evidence the private nature of ethical drives within social entrepreneurship. The individual's trajectory towards social entrepreneurship begins with a moment of self-discovery, often triggered by a deep personal malaise; it is followed by the use of a series of discursive tools to nurture and hone their social entrepreneurial subjectivity; and this both results in and is effected through a redefinition of profit. What emerges is a deeply individualised model of ethics, One that originates from introspection and finds ultimate form in personal attributes.

What are the consequences of this individualisation? The first is that social entrepreneurship requires converting as many people as possible, which is to say everyone, into a social entrepreneur. If 'changing the world' is an ethical objective that springs from individuals' will to express their own selves, it follows that, for the change to actually happen, a growing number of individuals have to develop a certain kind of self. In this respect, social entrepreneurship is first and foremost an identitarian movement.

This is evident in social entrepreneurship literature. William Drayton, founder of Ashoka, the largest global association supporting social entrepreneurship, makes this clear by arguing that when everyone is a changemaker, the problems can no longer outrun the solutions (Drayton, 2006a, 2006b). Ashoka's mission, indeed, is expressed in the trademark slogan 'Everyone is a Changemaker™'. In the *Global Education Magazine*, Drayton writes that:

> The first step to an 'Everyone is a Changemaker™' world is believing that you can make lasting change and acting on your belief. Identify a problem in your community and give yourself permission to overcome it. Once you enact change, once you internalize that you are a changemaker, you grow in confidence to tackle bigger problems. Each new problem is an opportunity for you to express love and respect in action at the highest possible level. Our world will transform as a result.
>
> (Drayton, 2012)

Drayton's words articulate a discourse in which the change has to be acted by individuals on themselves: you have to believe that 'you can make lasting change'; you have to have the 'confidence to tackle bigger problems'. The successful actualisation of this belief is conceived of as depending again on the action of individuals on themselves. It is a matter of 'giving yourself permission'. Once this first step has been taken, the changemaker identity gets internalised. At that point, 'changing the world' becomes an opportunity to 'express' your virtuous feelings of love and respect. The world will then become a better place, 'as a result'. From this perspective, global change depends upon changes in an individuals' subjectivity. What emerges is a vision in which 'change' is a result or a sort of osmosis or 'virality' that will make everyone a social entrepreneur. Drayton writes that:

> As the number of local changemakers increases, barriers are replaced by support institutions and respect, which encourages yet more family, friends, and neighbours to step up and take on other challenges.
>
> (Drayton, 2007: 49)

Social entrepreneurship ethical proposals are dependent upon the ability to produce an increasing number of social entrepreneurial subjects, or changemakers, as Ashoka labels them. The logic is cogent: since changing the world depends upon changing individuals' subjectivity, it is this very subjectivity that must be multiplied, as if in a democratisation and ideologisation of Schumpeter's entrepreneurial spirit. The Richard Florida utopia of a society where 'everyone is creative' (Florida, 2002) is replaced by One where 'everyone is a changemaker'.

Evidently, the claim that 'everyone is a changemaker' implies that there must be a way for everyone to become such, to 'become who you are' (to draw on a psychological new age parlance, where 'becoming' is a matter of expressing One's authenticity). What is involved is the process of 'unleashing', 'untapping' and 'releasing' that has characterised the discourse about self-actualisation in neoliberal societies. This process is essential for the individual to be able to set up a social enterprise. Indeed, before having an 'impact' on society, One must act upon oneself. Through this reflexive action, social entrepreneurs aspirants are meant to develop the correct subjectivity from which the social business can arise.

This implies that the self has to be consulted and interrogated, with the enterprise ideally emerging out of a process of self-enquiry. Indeed, the process of setting up a social enterprise is often narrated as a personal adventure, which culminates in the transformation of the self. In this regard, I quote Debora Szebeko, founder of Think Public – a London-based social enterprise[1] – who, while giving a PowerPoint presentation about the journey she has gone through to finally set up her enterprise, marked the moment of success with an exemplary slide declaring: 'Now you are a business!'

This is indicative of the dialectical relationship between the business and the self, where the first originates from the latter and vice versa. Hence, it must emerge spontaneously out of an inherently creative self. And if 'everyone is a changemaker' and every individual can develop a business by actualising itself, it follows that there must be a business for every self. Social entrepreneurs aspirants have to judiciously identify the core business that suits their own personality: 'The world abounds with noble causes, and there is One that is just right for you', as a popular book claims (Scofield, 2011: 5).

To develop an entrepreneurial personality means to be capable of bringing forth those parts of the self in a way that they can be framed in the form of the enterprise. The sets of personality questions we encountered earlier are meant to lead the individual to identify, highlight and articulate the parts that can be actualised in the form of the social enterprise. Practically, it corresponds to being able to translate and formalise personal values and virtues into a business plan. Producing subjectivity does not therefore only require cultivating generic characteristics, such as self-confidence, resilience, and performative flair, as we encountered in the previous chapter. But it also requires honing the material of the self in a unique manner to discover One's correspondingly unique business.

A consequence of this is a model of social enterprise, which is to say a model of political problem solving, that rests upon the personalities, aspirations and judgements of individuals rather than the collective. Zygmunt Bauman has written extensively on the consequences of this kind of individualisation. In his essay 'Individually, Together', preface of Beck and Beck-Gernsheim's *Individualization*, he affirms that this necessarily excludes and closes up the space for social responsibility:

> The individual tends to be lukewarm, sceptical or wary of 'common good', 'good society' or 'just society'. What is the sense of 'common interests' except allowing each individual to satisfy his or her own? Whatever else individuals may do when coming together portends constraint on their freedom to pursue what they see fit for themselves and won't help such pursuits anyway.
>
> (Bauman, in Beck and Beck-Gernsheim, 2002: xviii)

The subjectivity of social entrepreneurs shows how the imperative to freely pursue what individuals see 'fit for themselves' can reintegrate the common good within its ends if it redefines this as part of individual expression. Social entrepreneurs who claim to pursue the common good (epitomised in the phrase 'changing the world') do not contrast this with their own personal satisfaction; rather, the two are made to coincide. Their discourses reveal a regime of truth in which the dimension concerning the other-than-itself is reintegrated in a fully individualised subjectivity, for it is deciphered as belonging to the sphere of self-interest. Therefore, while social entrepreneurship proposes a discourse whose objective is the common good, the character and origins of this remain constrained within the limits of the individual self.

RECKONING WITH THE INWARD TURN

The question of this chapter has centred around how the social entrepreneurial subjectivity reintegrates an ethical dimension within individualised and entrepreneurialised conduct. This chapter's answer has emerged from the personal narratives of individuals like Alfredo, Noemi and Sara. They, like the many others I talked with over eighteen months in London and Milan over tea, cocktails and canapés, had experienced deeply personal journeys into the world of social entrepreneurship. Each story was unique, and yet shared the same pattern: a deep dissatisfaction, in some cases depression, caused the individual to look inside themselves for a different source of meaning through ethics; they sought the expression of these ethics through social entrepreneurship; they used various discursive tools, such as how-to books, academic courses and materials provided in a place like Impact Hub, to hone their embryonic social entrepreneurial identity; this effected and required a redefinition of profit, whereby financial and ethical capital are reinterpreted as equally valuable and in need of equilibrium; and finally, the social enterprise begins to take shape through attending to One's own passions, experiences and aspirations. Social entrepreneurship thereby resolves the competing commands made upon the millennial subject: to make money doing good.

This narrative exposes what I have termed an ethical inward turn, whereby ethics emerges from self-inquiry rather than political analysis; from looking inwards rather than outwards. Social entrepreneurship is built on the notion of ethics as an individual's skill to be expressed, and entrepreneurial tools as the adequate and effective actualisers of the individual's ethical beliefs. This approach to ethical problem solving, in which the social enterprise is the instrument for 'changing the world', proposes entrepreneurial tools as ethically neutral. Individualising ethics devolves the realisation of a better society to the values and virtues of individuals who act autonomously, with little to no coordination, and with a set of assumptions about what constitutes a problem that is worth solving. This reintegration is effected by means of deciphering ethical ambitions as part of the individual's self that needs to be expressed.

NOTE

1. Think Public is a social enterprise whose 'mission' is to find 'creative solutions to big social challenges', and which lately has specialised in service design for the NHS (Think Public, 2016).

Chapter V

Flawed Re-Enchantment

Finding the Political in Neoliberal Societies

Social entrepreneurs tend to refuse the adjective 'political' to refer to their identity and actions. On the contrary, they display a harsh scepticism in regard to the mechanisms of representative democracies in contemporary western societies. Nevertheless, as we established in our definition of social entrepreneurship in chapter I, their activity is of a political character. They cannot but enter the terrain of the political if they are to identify and solve societal problems, two activities that are foundational to social entrepreneurship. Social entrepreneurs therefore simultaneously take up the mantle of the political while rejecting it – or at least a particular version of what it might mean.

How do social entrepreneurs perceive the political, and their activity in relation to it? What can be said about the politics of social entrepreneurs? This chapter explores social entrepreneurs' discourse, situating it within the wider rejection of traditional forms of politics in the neoliberal era. We will see how collective, party or parliamentary-based politics are conceived as inefficient and ineffective. In its place arises a solutionist model that desperately avoids the bureaucracy and contentious connotations of the 'political'. We will then explore the consequences of such a manoeuvre, whereby the market (rather than the electorate) becomes the ultimate site of veridiction for political strategies, which are constitutionally unable to address structural problems. What's more, collective action is sacrificed in favour of the individual social entrepreneur. By unravelling these consequences, it will be possible to recognise the ultimate limitations of the politics of social entrepreneurship.

What emerges is a model of politics that bears some of the traits of 'post-politics'. At stake there is an understanding of politics whereby disenchantment with traditional models of political action lead to a supposedly 'post-ideological' managerial logic of solutionism. At the same time, social entrepreneurs express an undeniable passion for acting for the improvement of society, and a profound dissatisfaction for some of the malaise of capitalism, that is, structural inequalities and the prominence of individual profit over common good. What emerges, therefore, is an impassioned response to the ennui of political disenchantment: a re-enchantment with politics (if by another name) in times of neoliberalism. In the context of a generation that has inherited the political failures of its parents', social entrepreneurs have found a spell with which to re-enchant themselves with the zest and fever of political hope – albeit a constitutionally limited One. Hearing from several entrepreneurs, it's possible to observe the flourishing of political ambition, which takes the form of a local and a-systemic 'solution' to disillusionment with politics.

THE POLITICS OF SOCIAL ENTREPRENEURSHIP

Social entrepreneurs express a fierce resentment towards political parties, to which they ascribe a series of historical failures. This reasoning reflects a wider mentality that devalues any form of bureaucratic apparatus in favour of localised and autonomous actions. If by the term 'politics', we mean the legislative and executive actions of a government within the institutions of the state, carried out by means of associations of people who are supposed to represent the interests of citizens, then social entrepreneurs can surely be defined as apolitical subjects. While it is impossible to fully generalise, virtually every research participant I met showed a similar mode of thinking about this matter, and the narratives of the field articulate a quite dismissive attitude towards what may be referred to as traditional politics. Typically, social entrepreneurs do not find themselves represented in any party.

Nonetheless, they mobilise a discourse concerned with 'impact' and 'change', assuming the right and responsibility to act with the aim of transforming and improving society. Solving a problem also entails identifying, defining and framing phenomena *as* problems, and prioritising them as worthy of solution. The framing of societal issues alters what kinds of interventions are possible and popularised, affecting who is helped and who is not. And so while social entrepreneurs may dismiss the category, they participate in the field of political action.

I deploy the term 'political' in its anthropological sense, which leaves aside the institutional character of politics in favour of an understanding that focuses on a more subjective dimension: to refer to a specific sphere of thinking, feeling and doing. Drawing on Foucault, I define it as the dimension concerning the analysis of 'what we are willing to accept in our world – to accept, to refuse, to change – both in ourselves and in our circumstances' (Foucault,

2007: 152). It is an understanding of politics as a mode of thought and action, and bypasses the operations of the state. In these terms, social entrepreneurial subjectivity is political for it produces discourses and practices concerned with how to effect a 'change', seeking to intervene in the affairs of the people and operating in the uncertain domain of the future. Notably, social entrepreneurs are often referred to as 'changemakers' or 'impact makers', and celebrated as those who can suggest a future path for a more just society.

As chapter IV has illustrated, social entrepreneurs conceive of work not only as a means for expressing talents and passions but also (and mostly) as values and virtues, which may relate to a political dimension. Their thinking is built on joining individuals' virtues and values with positive social impact: entrepreneurial means are conceived of as a sort of bridge between the two, as the tools for the actualisation of private virtues in the public sphere. Social entrepreneurship is also a way to make a living out of One's passions and virtues, to live for and off One's cause, thus creating the condition for vocation and profession to coincide. What social entrepreneurship shows is the spectacular and paradoxical marriage between business means and political ends. And so, even though social entrepreneurs mostly neglect the political character of their discourse, social entrepreneurship 'by its very nature is always already a political phenomenon' (Cho, 2006: 36).

A number of questions here emerge: What kind of politics is at stake? How is politics – intended as the will to 'change the world' – redefined when it is attempted through the means of entrepreneurship? How can this form of political action be described and defined? What are its substantial characteristics? And what are its wider practical and theoretical implications? This chapter tackles three key elements of social entrepreneurs' politics – the localisation and a-systemic nature of its solutions, the market as the site of their veridiction and the subordination of the collective's vision in favour of the individual's – before situating social entrepreneurship's politics within a wider context of political disenchantment.

THE MARKET AS THE SITE OF VERIDICTION OF POLITICAL ACTIONS

Federica, a twenty-eight-year-old woman of Italian and Swedish descent who lives in Milan, is working on an online platform for the crowdfunding of political causes. She graduated in media and communication at a prestigious university, and has always been active in the feminist movement. Over a veggie burger on her terrace, she told me that after having tried other ways of being involved in the politics of her city – that is, participation in social movements and activism in the left-wing party (or what is left of it) – she finally decided to become an entrepreneur: 'I wanted to have an impact, you know? And while entrepreneurial tools are quick and independent, traditional politics is caught up in bureaucracy and after a while of trying to deal with it, it just kills any enthusiasm'. Cosimo, an economics graduate from Milan in his early forties, echoes these remarks. He had worked for many years in an NGO, before funding a social enterprise consultancy firm in London. We had lunch together in a pub in Islington, famous for its roasts and delicious scotch eggs. While eating, we discussed the idea that social entrepreneurship could perhaps be seen as a form of politics, as a way of doing politics, although, of course, very different from traditional party politics. Cosimo said that if that was the case, then at stake there would have been 'a much better form of politics'! Recounting his experience at the NGO, he concluded that: 'If you work in partnership with governments you are never free, you have to follow directives, procedures, a whole set of rules that most of the time compromise the success of whatever you're trying to do.'

Federica, Paolo and Cosimo reproduce a discourse that characterises entrepreneurship as an opportunity to avoid state bureaucracy. The relationship between social entrepreneurs and entrepreneurial tools is configured as One between individuals who act beyond the 'obsolete' barriers of bureaucratic institutions and are driven by big ideals, and a series of effective means that represent a successful alternative to party politics and social movements. In this perspective, entrepreneurial means acquire the significance of effective enablers, of guarantors of efficiency and autonomy. Social entrepreneurs' attitude towards social change replicates the traits of what Eugeny Morozov calls 'solutionism'. In *To Save Everything Click Here*, Morozov analyses the ideology produced by technology and argues that it entails a mode of thinking that recasts 'all complex social situations either as neatly defined problems with definite, computable solutions or as transparent and self-evident processes that can be easily optimized' (Morozov, 2013: 30–31). Morozov uses the term 'solutionism' in an 'unabashedly pejorative' fashion to pinpoint its consequences:

> Herein lies One hidden danger of solutionism: the quick fixes it peddles do not exist in a political vacuum. In promising almost immediate and much cheaper results, they can easily undermine support for more ambitious, more intellectually stimulating, but also more demanding reform projects.
>
> (Morozov, 2013: 38)

Moreover, he argues, solutionism, while addressing One problem, may well cause many others, to which its inherent approach is inevitably blind for it is unable to focus on the modes in which 'problems are composed', interrelated and function in a wider system. Social entrepreneurs' politics can be regarded as an expression of the same ideology, an ideology that claims to be non-ideological, and supports this claim by focusing on the 'effectiveness' of the solutions, rather than on the elaboration of a systematic set of ideas on how a just society should be. This is evident in the claims about the effectiveness of entrepreneurship versus the ineffectiveness of political parties, often partnered up with dismissal of left and right. Here the notion of effectiveness functions as the main dispositive of the ideology of solutionism. In this mobilisation of the ideological signifier of 'effectiveness', the neoliberal genealogy of solutionism reveals itself. Indeed, the replacement of any qualitative criteria of judgement (political, moral, etc.) with measurable quantitative indicators is what characterises the neoliberal regime of truth.

As Davies put it:

> This technocratic turn diverts the attention of the liberal away from moral or political philosophy and towards more mundane technical and pragmatic concerns. Prosaic market institutions and calculative devices become the harbinger of unspoken liberal commitments.
>
> (Davies, 2014: 7)

This description of neoliberal mentality and governmentality echoes Foucault's arguments in *The Birth of Biopolitics*, where he analyses the political economy as the main 'intellectual instrument' of neoliberal governmentality (Foucault, 2010: 13). He argues that:

> Success and failure, rather than legitimacy and illegitimacy, are the criteria of evaluation of political economy. . . . Political economy reflects on governmental practices themselves, and it does not question them to determine whether or not they are legitimate in terms of right. It considers them in terms of their effects rather than their origins.
>
> (Foucault, 2010: 13–15)

Adherence to the ideology of effectiveness forces social entrepreneurs to submit their values the final judgement of the market, for basically an enterprise is an entity that operates within the market, and that must survive in it. What determines the failure or the success of a social entrepreneur's problem-solving actions is therefore the market mechanism. By translating political passion into business activities, the success of the latter becomes the only way to assess the value of the first. Quite simply, what if some very valid political strategies turn out to be not financially profitable? Bankruptcy or financial success becomes the ultimate criteria with which to judge the desirability and feasibility of ethical and political objectives. Social entrepreneurs, as well as commentators and promoters of social entrepreneurship, are not unaware of this. The efforts made to formulate a quantitative indicator for qualitative benefits are the basis of the research about the SROI (Social Return on

Investment) (i.e. Nicholls et al., 2009; Zappala and Lyons, 2009; Millar and Hall, 2012; Maier et al., 2015) which Nicholls defines as 'a framework for measuring and accounting for this much broader concept of value; it seeks to reduce inequality and environmental degradation and improve wellbeing by incorporating social, environmental and economic costs and benefits' (Nicholls et al., 2012: 8). In the UK, the network Social Value UK, founded in 2008, has the declared goal of changing 'the way society accounts for value' (Social Value UK, 2019). Social Venture Capital (SVC) funds, sometimes called Impact Funds, are supposed to invest according to these particular types of return. The world of SVC is growing. An article published in *Forbes* reads as follows:

> Some estimate that the impact investment market could grow to $3 trillion. And as the more socially-conscious millennial generation of entrepreneurs build impact-driven businesses, you can be sure the supply of impact investment opportunities will vastly expand.
>
> (Cohen and Bannik, 2014)

However, this is still insufficient to face and challenge the mainstream notion of economic value. It is beyond the scope of this book to assess the actual impact of SROI, or of Impact Funds. What is interesting in the perspective of this analysis is to highlight that within a neoliberal regime of truth that makes the market the site of veridiction of ethical and political instances, the lack of a measure, and the related attempts to measure the immeasurable, to quantify the unquantifiable, are the symptoms of social entrepreneurship ambivalence. In the lack of a measure of so-called social impact, and in the efforts to design One, resides the objectification of the philosophical clash between the ethics of profit and the ethics of the social. And it is a clash in which profit holds the upper hand: financial sustainability sets the conditions of existence for political aspirations.

LOCAL, A-SYSTEMIC POLITICS

Miranda is a British woman in her late twenties. She moved to London from the north of the country when she was nineteen. She graduated in architecture and in 2009 founded a social enterprise that aims at involving people in processes of social change by using the skill-set of participative design and architecture. With her projects, Miranda wants to fight social inequalities in the city of London. One of Miranda's projects concerned the transformation of a 'forgotten corner' of a Catford (South East London) school for children with disabilities 'into a new outdoor learn and play area'. She worked very closely with the school staff to plan a set of lessons in the existing space in order to observe how children engage with it. Through participant observation, she developed the idea of a set of coat hangers which can be used to transform the space into 'any theme for any learning objective'. Miranda has responded to the issue of structural inequality in neoliberal cities acting in a specific borough, in a specific school, with a very limited group of people.

Caterina is fashion designer based in Milan. A young woman in her mid-twenties, she feels part of a growing number of fashion designers who fiercely dislike the mainstream mode of production in the industry. She refuses the idea of fashion as mere consumerism; in fact, she claims she wants to fight consumerism itself. By means of her enterprise, Caterina reacts to this thinking by producing high quality and long-lasting shoes in a sustainable manner. In her small business, she does not replicate the patterns that she wants to fight in society: she works with local producers and high-quality material. Yet, her reach is limited: she employs an average of two people, on a freelance basis, and produces shoes, One of the massive number of goods that circulate in neoliberal free markets. Sara, who aims to change the system of re-education and reintegration of female prisoners and to reduce waste, is able to employ no more than ten inmates and to recycle a very limited quantity of fabric.

What I want to flag up with these observations is that small and medium enterprises can achieve only localised, circumscribed actions. Their agency is limited to specific phenomena, in specific places, involving specific people. To very big structural problems correspond localised and fractional actions.[1] What is striking is the relationship between a discourse that includes the vision of 'changing the world', and addresses very complex, deeply eradicated, social issues and an action that is necessarily localised. The form of action that social entrepreneurship carries out is inevitably limited to the sphere of immediate experience of individual entrepreneurs themselves. Consistently, it originates from the need to express the virtuous self, and the will to have a personal, measurable, impact as an individual.

I argue that what emerges is a form of experiential politics that disregards the systematic analysis of society to become an expression of individual virtues in the form of localised entrepreneurial action. I want to highlight that such action and discourse exclude the systemic and structural analysis of the causes of social issues. Instead, social entrepreneurship tends towards the isolation of the specific effects of a given political and economic paradigm. These effects get assessed in themselves rather than in relation to the wider geopolitical and economic matrix. The analysis and critique of neoliberal political economy that produces social inequality is virtually absent from the discourse of those who are tackling its symptoms by devising local solutions.

The young fashion designers who, like Caterina, are against consumerism and exploitation would hardly embark on an analysis of the mode of production and division of labour in the financial, globalised economy. They experience some consequences of it, in a rather immediate way, and in an even more immediate manner try to intervene in their sphere of influence. Caterina may well sell durable handmade shoes to express her dissent with the mainstream fashion industry, but this form of intervention cannot address the global distribution of power and the global price of labour that are the structural causes of the problems of the fashion industry she wants to tackle in the first place. These exceed her sphere of experience and intervention and therefore cannot be addressed by means of an enterprise.

The same applies to those who try to tackle inequality. Miranda does this by acting within the scope of her personal experience: dealing with its effects in a local school. The fact that following her intervention that school has new coat hangers that permit children to express their creativity, and has involved them in a process of co-design that increased their confidence, is surely a valuable output. Nonetheless, it will hardly change, or impact upon, the politics of education in the UK.

It is not that social entrepreneurs do not use data and value analysis at all, but their analysis is acted out by means of business in the market field. In a market, the use of data is about finding effective solutions to specific problems, which can survive only if they prove to be financially sustainable, that is, by attracting enough customers and capital. Sara's critical reflection on the way in which the Italian legal system punishes thieves, and on how the organisation of life in prison does not serve the purpose of the re-education of inmates, ultimately takes the form of a business model. Social problems translate into market opportunities. This, in the most successful cases, may even lead to the attenuation of some of the effects that the problem causes. However, the context of that problem, and the structural causes of the social issue addressed, cannot be affected. On the contrary, the introduction of the enterprise as a social actor reiterates the primacy of market principles rather than questioning them.

In this respect, social entrepreneurship is a form of politics that is entirely acted out at the place of the personal. It is through the experience of the direct effects of One's action that social entrepreneurs perceive themselves as having an impact. Politics becomes a matter of sheer experience. The straightforward recompense of immediate impact becomes the sign of an action that matters. Importantly, this experiential conception of politics is closely related with the conception of social and political change rooted upon individual, personal change (see chapter V). To the hermeneutic of the subject as the main instrument of change corresponds an experiential notion of politics.

Deciphered as a political paradigm, this implies a notion of change and political action that is totally dependent upon the utopic assumption that a very large number of individuals will eventually decide to set up similarly ethical businesses. In other words, the world cannot change unless all fashion designers design ethical garments. Unless in every prison there are enough social enterprises to employ each and every inmate. Unless an army of architects redesigns the entire suburbs of contemporary urban centres with the help of the community. The not-so-hidden utopia of social entrepreneurship is that everybody can (and will, and wants to) be a 'changemaker'. This structural change depends upon individuals' thoughts and actions. What we are confronted with is an idea of change as a sort of osmotic mimesis, which can be thought of as a form of virality: change is thought to happen through a gradual and subtle absorption of a mode of being and thinking that is supposed to spread rapidly by means of people communicating with each other.

INDIVIDUAL OVER THE COLLECTIVE

The individualism of the politics of social entrepreneurship is evident in its suppression of any form of trust or subjugation to collective organisation. Immediate experience acquires its importance because of, and in reaction to, the fading-out of the belief in any form of general will, social contract and – I would add – social and political science. This distinctive character of social entrepreneurship's politics is evident when compared with the political engagement that distinguished the party, an organisation that up until the sixties was considered a well-equipped instrument to effect social change.

In this regard, the autobiography of the British historian and lifelong communist Eric Hobsbawm may provide a useful term for comparison. Indeed, it can help to further grasp the significance of social entrepreneurship as revelatory of a shift in the mode in which political passion is conceived of and exercised. What emerges from Hobsbawm's accurate and passionate account is the position of the individual in relation to the party. The party was the One through which individuals believed it was possible to achieve a change in society. It was through submitting to the party line that people felt able to have an impact.

> The Party (we always thought of it in capital letters) had the first, or more precisely, the only real claim on our lives. Its demands had absolute priority. We accepted its discipline and hierarchy. We accepted the absolute obligation to follow 'the line' it proposed to us, even when we disagreed with it, although we made heroic efforts to convince ourselves of its intellectual and political 'correctness' in order to 'defend it', as we were expected to.
>
> (Hobsbawm, 2002: 201)

This almost unconditional submission was necessary and legitimate as the party was thought to be the only organisation powerful enough to address large scale social facts (e.g. inequality or the balance of the world economy) and therefore to obtain structural change on a grand scale. Such a degree of submission to the party is well encapsulated in the famous sentence of Enrico Berlinguer: 'men [*sic*] can make mistakes, but the Party never does.' Bianca Berlinguer, his daughter and established journalist, comments on these words as follows:

> We need to remember that this sentence is indicative of the fact that the party appeared as . . . a superior entity . . . because it represented the tool to pursue a project, an ideal, a dream . . . a collective project in which both the leaders and the militants would identify completely because the fundamental principle of militancy was that individuals' redemption happened through the collective's. . . . To the party, people would dedicate their life.
>
> (Berlinguer, 2015: min 06:00)

While Eric Hobsbawm's and Enrico Berlinguer's engagement with the communist party might be extreme examples, they are revelatory of a mode of political being that distinguished most modern politics. The focal point is the understanding of individuals' political action as necessarily going through collective action. Social entrepreneurs represent a reversal of this relation: it is collective action that must go through an individual's One. If in modern politics, individuals' will must pass through subjugation to the collective will (e.g. the will of the party), contemporary social entrepreneurs bear the traits of a politics where it is collective will that must pass through individuals' will to be eventually realised.

Paolo Virno's analysis of the multitude may help to conceptualise this shift in the relationship between the individual and the collective. In his short and brilliant book *A Grammar of the Multitude*, he provides an account that rejects the simplistic alternatives of enthusiastic exaltation or sheer condemnation in regard to individualism. Rather, he offers a nuanced and complex analysis that faces, instead of hiding, the inner ambiguities of the contemporary subject. He defines contemporary forms of life through the concept of multitude. Drawing on Hobbes, a fierce critic of this notion and advocate of its opposite, that is, the 'people', he describes the multitude as the 'social and political existence of the many, seen as being many' (Virno, 2004: 22). This formulation highlights the constitutional incapacity of the many to converge into a One – e.g. the party, the state or any other organisation whose function is to subsume individuals' will. It was the structural incapacity of the multitude to effect this 'transfer' that caused Hobbes' repugnance. Indeed, he saw it as what 'did not make itself fit into people' and 'contradicts the state monopoly of political decision making' (Virno, 2004: 24). While the 'people' are the form of life of representative democracy, the form of life that delegates to a supposedly superior organ the actualisation of their political and moral rights, the multitude refuses any form of subjugation to a 'sovereign' other than their very self.

This synthetic, but precise, description well defines the subjectivity of social entrepreneurs. What they are incapable of and unwilling to do is to subsume their passion, will, and desire, to a bigger entity. Their regime of truth is built on the affirmation of the failure of any action conducted by means of big political organisations.[2] Yet, Virno explains, the fact that the multitude does not converge into a One does not mean that they have got rid of the One. It rather implies a variation on the positioning of the One in respect of the many. Instead of being that into which the many converge, as was the case for the people, for the multitude the One represents a common point of departure. What is 'common/shared' is not a form of general representation of individuals' wills, rather their origin.

I believe this further characterisation of the multitude may be valuable to comprehending the subjectivity of social entrepreneurs. What they are united by is their social entrepreneurial subjectivity. Their One is the acceptance of a common regime of truth that embraces a form of individualised ethics, and the notion of entrepreneurial means as an effective method to intervene in society. The common thread that unites social entrepreneurs is the tautological evidence of having/developing a social entrepreneurial self. Then, the modes in which this gets actualised, the modes in which ethics becomes politics, are diverse and independent from each other in their content and focus.

SOCIAL ENTREPRENEURSHIP AS A POST-POLITICAL PHENOMENON

In this chapter, we've seen how social entrepreneurs business enterprise assumes the role of traditional political tools as a means to change the world. In social entrepreneurship, immediate impact has taken the place of structural change as a definition of what changing the world entails. Its entrepreneurial form imposes the translation of social analysis into a business model that turns social issues into market gaps to be addressed by means of a business. This has at least three interrelated consequences: the first is the individualistic dimension of the political action; the second is the vision of society as 'something to be fixed' and the consequent reduction of politics to problem solving; the third is that the market becomes the site of verification of political actions.

Social entrepreneurship politics may be understood as a form of post-political thought. Post-politics involves the suppression of the political in favour of a managerial logic that dismisses ideology to promote technocratic decision-making (Wilson and Swyngedouw, 2014). One of its main traits is a post-ideological ideology, that is, the ideological belief in the end of all ideologies. As Slavoj Žižek puts it:

> Post-politics thus emphasizes the need to leave old ideological visions behind and confront new issues, armed with the necessary expert knowledge and free deliberation that takes people's concrete needs and demands into account.
> (Žižek, 1999: 198)

What is erased together with the recognition of the ideological aspects of political thought and action is the antagonistic character of the political. As argued by Chantal Mouffe, an antagonistic character is indispensable for an understanding and practice of the political if it is to recognise the plurality of opinions, needs and ideas within the democratic arena (Mouffe, 2005). The intention to go 'beyond left and right', to quote a famous book by Anthony Giddens, ultimately results in the reduction of different worldviews to the allegedly incontestable level of utility (Mouffe, 2005). This way, political choice is de facto eliminated and replaced by the perception of sheer necessity. A consequence of this is the disenchantment of citizens, who lose confidence in their ability to change the status quo by means of their right to vote.

Social entrepreneurship's constitutional absence of systemic thought and analysis results in the dismissal of any form of traditional political ideology (e.g. the difference between left and right). What's more, the election of the enterprise as a method to devise effective solutions to social problems entails the acceptance that the market is the ultimate site of veridiction for political actions. The acceptance of the inevitability of capitalism, which produces and is produced by the progressive deterioration of trust in democratic processes and institutions, is One of the defining features of this spirit.

Social entrepreneurs show a post-political sensibility to the extent that they express scepticism towards democratic political institutions, deemed as 'slow', 'bureaucratic' and 'ineffective'. Moreover, rather than challenging neoliberalism – especially where it elevates the market as the ultimate criterion of verification of ethical and political actions – they tend to distinguish between a 'good' and a 'bad' capitalism. This is evident in the attempt to redefine profit as instrumental for the achievement of the collective good (see chapter V).

The solutionism of social entrepreneurship reflects this vision in so far as it addresses social issues as problems to be solved, bypassing the discussion of the genealogy of those problems, and therefore their political origin. Through the notion of post-politics, this can be explained as an effect of the process of depoliticisation that, by eliminating the conflict of ideology, isolates effectiveness as the final and sole parameter for decision-making. This way, actions are evaluated on how they 'work well within the framework of existing relations' (Žižek, 1999: 199). But, as Slavoj Žižek argues: 'the political act is not simply something that works well within the framework of the existing relations, but something that changes the very framework that determines how things work' (Žižek, 1999: 199). Ultimately, the regime of truth of social entrepreneurship produces and is produced by a post-political mode of acting and thinking that reduces politics to the administration of things, and that is unable to fully challenge the neoliberal market. Instead, it makes it the litmus test of its success and value.

RE-ENCHANTMENT THROUGH THE ENTERPRISE

We have seen how social entrepreneurs, driven by a disenchantment with collective and institutional forms of political action, wholeheartedly reject the term 'political'. They subordinate the political to the economic calculus of the market. The exclusion of moral and political rights and values from the process of evaluation of social policies is what William Davies refers to as 'the disenchantment of politics by economy' (Davies, 2014: 1). He argues that:

> The central defining characteristic of all neoliberal critique is its hostility to the ambiguity of political discourse, and a commitment to the explicitness and transparency of quantitative, economic indicators, of which the market price system is the model. Neoliberalism is the pursuit of the disenchantment of politics by economics.
>
> (Davies, 2014: 13)

Social entrepreneurship is characterised by these features of disenchantment, for it ultimately poses the market and its quantifiable indicators as the site of veridiction of actions that retain or emerge from political ambitions.

Yet, social entrepreneurs are certainly not generally disillusioned. Their passion is remarkable. Take Miranda, whom I introduced at the beginning of the chapter. She is an architecture graduate but has never looked for a job in a studio; over a banana and strawberry juice whose label promises it does not contain any preservatives, she explained to me:

> Why continue to design ever higher buildings? What for? In the end, it's just a thing to nourish the architects' ego. I am not interested in designing galleries or museums to show off how skilled I am. . . . I rather want to use my expertise to improve the world, not to make it worse with yet another skyscraper!

After years of struggle, working part-time in pubs and restaurants, and volunteering to build her portfolio, Miranda funded her business which at the time had only One employee: herself. Now she still runs that business, and has six employees. She and her team keep on delivering participative design projects in various disadvantaged areas across London. Like many of the social entrepreneurs whose voices are part of this research, her motivations exceed the sphere of self-interest, and they originate from the will to intervene in society to fight inequalities:

> I did not want the life of people to be determined by their postcode. If you grow up in a disadvantaged area you are surrounded by poor buildings and ill-designed spaces, and spending time in poor housing or in low quality schools creates a huge psychological barrier that prevents people getting access to better spaces. It's about equality, and equal opportunities.

Miranda has made substantial sacrifices to realise her vision of a better society, taking personal and financial risks to do so.

Caterina has a different background and nationality from Miranda, but she shares a similar vision. She designs, produces and sells shoes, and to explain her motivations for doing it, she mobilises a narrative that combines the need for self-expression with the will to have a positive impact on society. On a hot July afternoon, she welcomed me to her studio, in an upper-class residential borough of Milan. It used to be her mother's accounting studio, but now it's her own. As if to offer justification for the elegant space she occupies, she smiled and declared: 'I do all of this because I like it . . . to express myself!' As we have seen, when it comes to social entrepreneurs, self-expression goes along with the will to 'change the world'. In the case of Caterina, this operates in the world of fashion:

> When I was studying fashion design for my MA, I couldn't stand the idea of fashion held by my professors and fellow students! A fashion made of unwearable clothes, cheap garments, things that you end up throwing out after a few months! And on top of this, everything is produced in developing countries, basically exploiting their labour force! This is unacceptable, totally unacceptable and must change!

To actively contribute to achieve this change, Caterina tries to do 'things differently': 'Everything I produce is made in Italy, I give work to Tuscany leather artisans, I produce a shoe that lasts for years, that goes against consumerist ideology!' She claims that she feels part of a 'bigger movement' of young people who do not want to live in 'the consumerist society' because 'it is a way of living that is dying, that is not sustainable and must change'. Caterina makes shoes with this big picture in mind, it is not only about business but also about being part of 'a yet to come revolution'. Sara, who the reader may remember from this chapter, set up a social enterprise that offers work to female prisoners and produces shopping bags by recycling fabric waste. For her, the issues to be tackled are waste, integration and education. This is how she frames her decision and describes her activities:

> I had been volunteering in Asia for a month. I was working in a community house, we organised distance adoptions, I saw a striking reality: all these kids . . . and I was helping them . . . then I thought well, how can I act for the common good? Once back to Italy I thought: female prisoners and waste products, because the state treats inmates as human waste. . . . These people spend twenty hours in a cell, to the citizens they cost 400 euro per day, and when they get out they are angrier than before, and they have not learnt anything. Then I imagined the amazing number of free hours . . . free hours that become endless, and then they take drugs to sleep . . . and it's crazy because the Italian law condemns them to 3 years for theft, and 15 years for five thefts . . . for a theft we pay 400 euro per day for three years, and when she gets out, older and angrier . . . god knows what she'll do then! I have a woman who works for me, with the salary she receives she got a mortgage to buy a house, she is able to send her kid to school. . . . When she comes out of prison she'll have a house and a son who's integrated in this country. . . . You know . . . paradoxically, from inside prison she's helping those outside. . . . And then I also help all of those textile warehouses that need to get rid of fabric waste. . . . They are so happy because they dispose of waste, and make donations, so we all win!

The discourses of these women are indicative of a deep dissatisfaction with the way in which society is organised, and they take into account some of the issues that are an integral part of the political debate: inequality, exploitation and discrimination. Miranda is fully aware that the property market and urban planning of the UK creates structural inequality, Caterina fiercely criticises the mode of production of the global fashion industry, and Sara's thinking is built on the recognition of a fault within the enforcement of the law in her country.

Miranda, Caterina and Sara are concerned with an aspect of society that they consider unjust, unsustainable and unethical. With their businesses, they want to impact on some structural, long-term, very complex social issues, that is, inequality, the organisation of labour in the fashion industry and the judicial apparatus that regulates punishment. The end of their action is reduced neither to the design of a service or product, nor to monetary return. In fact, these originate from an (individualised) ethical sensitivity and get actualised to concretely fight specific social issues.

Social entrepreneurs may be seen as reacting to neoliberal political disenchantment by reintegrating political passions and ideas within their discourse and actions. As is evident in the frequent mobilisation of the emphatic formula 'changing the world', social entrepreneurs seem to be enchanted by the opportunity to be political actors. They exhibit a determined passion for improving society that is borne out in major life decisions, which often involve substantial risks. In this respect, they emulate a previous generation of political activists. Where they differ is the employment of entrepreneurial means, deference to market logic, the localisation of their efforts, and the primacy of the individual over the collective. What they get in return for these tactics is an income, an experienciable impact and greater personal autonomy. Social entrepreneurs experiential and a-systemic (post-)politics can be seen as emerging in the space left available by the disenchantment of neoliberalism. At stake, there is the attempt to readdress political sentiments within neoliberal governmentality and ideology.

THE RE-ENCHANTMENT OF SOCIAL ENTREPRENEURSHIP

This chapter has concentrated on the politics of social entrepreneurship. It has demonstrated that social entrepreneurs, although individualised neoliberal subjects, express a form of political passion in so far as they are concerned with the discourses and practices of change, in the aim of creating a better future. Importantly, they do so by means of business enterprise, which have replaced traditional political means as a tool to transform and improve society. This replacement reflects a profound distrust in the functioning of the state and government, and a mutated political sensitivity which is rooted in and confined to the domain of personal experience and influence.

Social entrepreneurs can therefore be credited with finding a means of political re-enchantment. But its imagination of political possibility is constitutionally limited. By mobilising the notion of effectiveness as the principal criteria of decision-making and rejecting the distinction between conflicting ideologies, they remain confined to a post-political dimension that precludes the emergence of proper 'political acts', that is, those acts that can change social and economic systems. Social entrepreneurship could therefore be characterised as neoliberalism's recuperation of political hope in a form that strengthens the primacy of the market. But equally we could look from the perspective of Miranda, Caterina, Sara and other social entrepreneurs working with flawed mechanisms and limited resources who seek to improve society, in some cases through many years of personal and financial struggle. This is not to sentimentally celebrate the social entrepreneur, but to mark the kind of political enchantment that can survive in conditions of neoliberalism.

The theoretical and practical effects of such form of post-politics must be evaluated in future research, as it is still too soon to empirically assess all its connotations. Moreover, social entrepreneurship is a culture in the making and any absolute claim in its regard would crystallise a reality that is *in fieri*. However, some reflections can be made. In the conclusion, we will expand on some points to highlight how the analysis of social entrepreneurship can help us to better understand the contemporary neoliberal zeitgeist.

NOTES

1. Big corporations have an impact that may well be global and involve a large number of people. However, this does not apply to the social entrepreneurs who are part of this study, whose means and resources are limited. Also, there is a problem with the scalability of social enterprise, as when an enterprise grows, it is much more difficult to combine the economic and social aspect. Scalability is a much discussed topic in academic as well as popular literature (Dudnik, 2010; Smith et al., 2013; Gabriel, 2014) and One of the main concerns of the more established social entrepreneurs I have met (i.e. during a roundtable at Social Enterprise London, organised to bring together social entrepreneurs from Italy and the UK, the issue of scale emerged strongly).

2. Such negative conceptions of modern political organs constitute the core of the reflexive narratives of the field, and are supported by most of the academic literature on the topic (see chapter I). For instance, Gregory Dees, author of the seminal article 'The Meaning of Social Entrepreneurship', states that 'many governmental and philanthropic efforts have fallen far short of our expectations. Major social sector institutions are often viewed as inefficient, ineffective, and unresponsive. Social entrepreneurs are needed to develop new models for a new century' (Dees, 2001: 1).

Conclusion

Future after Future: Social Entrepreneurs and the Changemaker Generation

Alfredo spent about two years trying to launch his social enterprise. He invested practically all the savings he had to support himself in London while attending networking events, conferences, workshops and meet-ups, in the aim of branding himself as a changemaker and to gain a reputation in the field. For in order to attract investors, you have to be recognised by the 'community' of peers as someone who can 'have an impact' (Bandinelli and Arvidsson, 2013). In 2013, to get some visibility and feedback, he even funded a pilot project with some money he inherited from his family. In those months, Alfredo was dedicating all his time to his business, mostly displaying an enthusiastic (maybe overenthusiastic) attitude: 'We are going to change the world!' he would repeat, perhaps as a way to reassure himself of the ethical rationality of his financially irrational choices.

Eventually, Alfredo's start-up failed. Statistically, that was not surprising, for about 90 per cent of start-ups fail within a couple of years (Patel, 2015). Despite the plethora of how-to books and university degrees, to be successful as an entrepreneur is quite a difficult thing. This is even truer in the scene that I researched, where the majority of enterprises are characterised by the absence of capital and the presence of only One employee, that is, the funder. Zero-capital enterprises and One-person enterprises represent the most common form of work organisation in the culture industries, and may be seen as the formal translation of knowledge workers' need to do the work of the structure themselves (McRobbie, 2002). At stake are immensely precarious ventures, which are unlikely to be sustainable, despite the good intentions of the funders.

Alfredo eventually had to find a job in a big corporation to make a living. However, he still thinks of himself as a social entrepreneur. Despite the commitment requested at work, he has found the time to run a weekly documentary screening night in Peckham (South-East London) and to manage a Facebook page for Italian social entrepreneurs. Moreover, he has kept on participating to various events in the scene, and organised two open workshops on social return on investment and on blockchain technologies. Currently, he is collaborating with his partner to the management of a 'café-coworking-hub' in Bricklane (East London). While working for a company, Alfredo dedicates a lot of his time to a myriad of activities whose perceived goal is that of 'making a change'. For him, as for many others, social entrepreneurship hasn't proved to be a feasible profession, but it has provided a source of meaning.

Giovanni, Elisa and Emily are a group of three friends of mine. We all live in the same area, at the boundary between Deptford and Greenwich, in South East London. After having completed their MAs, they have all gone through the process of finding a job. They worked for free for a few months, complying with the rules of the game that wants new graduates to do at least a couple of unpaid internships, but after two years, they were still practically unemployed. Elisa and Emily opted for a 'dull job' in cafes and restaurants. Giovanni worked as a sale assistant for a while, then he quit; he lives out of renting two family properties. A year ago, they started an 'upcycling' project called FabFabrics, whose core activity is to re-use waste material to create new products such as handbags, computer cases and plant-pot covers. Over the last months, they have worked on a new website, they improved their products and tried to sell them in a couple of local markets. Eventually, they registered as a social enterprise. Yet, so far, they have sold just a few items and are struggling to come up with a sustainable business strategy. But they keep on working on it. When I asked them why, they all referred to the frustrations of doing a 'boring', 'meaningless' and 'shitty' job, and the consequent decision to dedicate their time to something 'meaningful' to a 'job with a cause'.

For many people like Alfredo, Giovanni, Emily and Elisa, setting up an enterprise 'with a cause' is primarily a way to find meaning and purpose in a society that seems to have no more on offer than 'bullshit jobs' (Graeber, 2018) and the perspective of human extinction. As Adam Arvidsson suggests, 'changemaking' – in its various forms of which social entrepreneurship is One of the most diffused – has become a common aspiration, and even if the auspicated 'change' is rather vague, it still works to convince yourself that 'you are doing something valuable and that your life has a meaning' (Arvidsson, 2019: 4). In this light, social entrepreneurs may be seen as epitomising an emerging trend which sees the resignification of work as a means for the implementation of values and virtues. Recently, several pieces of research on creative workers have shown how ethical motivations, that is, motivations related to the improvements of society and of self, are likely to overcome financial Ones (McRobbie et al., 2016; Gandini et al., 2017). Work seems to have become an ethical and existential route, a matter of turning oneself into a specific subject.

Although this may not be something altogether new, in contemporary societies, we can see its gradual crystallisation. Organisations of various kinds are forming the infrastructure for this new ethos of production. Probably, the most representative unit of this ecosystem are coworking spaces. Typically branded as aimed at 'bringing the social back to work', they offer a cheap working station for precarious freelancers, while providing them with the tools to enact a certain ethos and become a certain kind of person (Bandinelli and Gandini, 2019; Bandinelli, 2019). Coworking spaces are reshaping the organisation of work in cities across the globe, along the lines of a communitarian and collaborative approach (Arvidsson, 2019).

Global cities are also increasingly populated of healthy-organic-authentic food retailers and independent-sustainable shops. Even in big supermarkets, it is plenty of brands that associate themselves with an ethical cause, so that it is increasingly difficult to find One that does not claim to have some sort of positive impact somewhere in the world. Awareness of the structural inequalities of the global labour market translates in more accurate consumption choices, supported by the cultural and economic capital of educated middle classes in urban centres. At stake, there is a generation that responds to political and economic disillusionment with a revival of ethics by means of styles of consumption.

It is hard to predict whether these emerging phenomena will actually lead to a change. For sure, as Arvidsson, 2019 argues, they are indicative of the fact that a cultural shift has happened since the institutions and infrastructures of capitalism are crumbling over the weight of financial precarity, inequality and ecological disasters. The vague future of social entrepreneurs and changemakers in general is a kind of 'future after future': it derives from and reacts to an underlying sense of loss of the future. Arguably, the future got lost with the end of the grand-narratives of modernity – the last of which was the myth of endless economic growth – and with them, of the ability to plan, whether at a social or personal level.

This kind of future can thus be interpreted as a reaction to, or a result of, the cultural death of the future. Put differently, it occupies the only space left vacant by the collapse of the possibility of imagining a future. To this extent, it signals what is still possible to imagine, while indicating the factors that have made this possibility possible, while making other possibilities impossible. What is possible, I suggest, is to think of a politics which is rooted on finding immediate solutions to present problems. It is a politics whose temporality is an ever-refreshing present. In this context, it is highly significant to look at what is left of the idea of the future.

Social entrepreneurs provide a case study to answer this question. They embody the neurotic split of the contemporary subject, who knows something has to change but doesn't know exactly how to change it. To express it in terms of a vignette: the contemporary subject is stuck in the paradoxical position of One who is watching a documentary on climate change, on a MacBook Pro assembled by exploited workers, eating a chicken breast full of hormones, which has been cooked using fossil fuel, and purchased in a supermarket that has been reached driving a car that needs petrol to work, and whose owners may well invest in toxic derivatives. Social entrepreneurs represent the struggle of a subject that is caught in a short circuit marked by the lacerating awareness that to ensure their own life they should stop living the only life they know. This antithesis does not find a further development in a political dialectic but has its sole resolution in the attempt to find meaning while possibly making a living and finding a quantum of solace in ethical consumption. They are brave enough to dare to talk about the future with confidence and optimism. But what is at stake seems to be the obsessive neurosis of a subject who keeps on acting on single issues as a way to escape from the real political question: How to think of a viable alternative political and economic paradigm?

Social entrepreneurs are very aware of this contradiction. The ethnographers who think they have understood something of their research participants which they don't already know is ingenuous at best. In June 2016, I presented some of the findings of this research to an audience comprised mostly social entrepreneurs, in the context of two events in Turin and Milan. Both presentations ended up with a lively and passionate debate on how to break through the iron cage of neoliberal capitalism. Quite a few people talked openly about their struggle of surviving in the market, and were very vocal about the precarious financial conditions, which they indicate as what prevents them to get organised in collective forms of political action. The question is still open: How to think of the end of capitalism disjoined from the end of the world?

Bibliography

Acemoglu, D. K. and Robinson, J. A. (2006) *Economic Origins of Dictatorship and Democracy*, Cambridge: Cambridge University Press.

ACRE (2007) *Milan City Region Is Still Competitive? Pathways to Creative and Knowledge-Based Regions*, Amsterdam: University of Amsterdam.

Adkins, L. and Lury, C. (1999) 'The Labour of Identity: Performing Identities, Performing Economies', in *Economy and Society*, 28(4), pp. 598–614.

Adler, P. (2006) *Whatever You Think Think the Opposite*, London: Penguin.

Agamben, G. (1998) *Homo Sacer: Sovereign Power and the Bare Life*, Stanford, CA: Stanford University Press.

Alvord, S. H., L. D. Brown and C. W. Letts (2004) 'Social Entrepreneurship and Societal Transformation: An Explanatory Study', in *The Journal of Applied Behavioural Science*, 40(3), pp. 260–83.

Annas, J. (2011) *Intelligent Virtue*, New York: Oxford University Press.

Arendt, A. (1998) *The Human Condition*, Chicago: University of Chicago Press.

Aristotle (2010) *Ethica Nicomachea*, Whitefish, MT: Kessinger Publishing.

Ardvisson, A. and Peitersen, N. (2013) *The Ethical Economy: Rebuilding Value after the Crisis*, New York: Columbia University Press.

Arvidsson, A., Malossi, G. and Naro, S. (2010) 'Passionate Work? Labour Conditions in the Milan Fashion Industry', in *Journal for Cultural Research*, 14(3), pp. 295–309.

Arvidsson, A. (2014) 'Public Brands and the Entrepreneurial Ethics', in *Ephemera*, 14(1), pp. 119–124.

Arvidsson, A., Gandini, A. and Bandinelli, C. (2016) 'Self-Branding among Freelance Knowledge Workers', in Crain, M. G., Poster, W. R. and Cherry, M. A. (eds.) *Invisible Labor: Hidden Work in the Contemporary Word*, Oakland: University of California Press, pp. 239–257.

Arvidsson, A. (2006) *Brands, Meaning and Value in Media Culture*, London: Routledge.

Arvidsson A (2019) *Changemakers: The Industrious Future of the Digital Economy*, Cambridge: Polity.

Ashoka (2016a) *Ashoka*. Available at: http://uk.ashoka.org/ (Accessed: 25 Sept. 2016).

Ashoka (2016b) *Everyone a Changemaker*. Available at: http://uk.ashoka.org/everyone-changemaker (Accessed: 3 Jun. 2016).

Ashoka (2016c) *What Is a Social Entrepreneur?* Available at: https://www.ashoka.org/social_entrepreneur (Accessed: 1 Jun. 2016).

Ashton, R. (2011) *How to Be a Social Entrepreneur: Make Money & Change the World*, Chichester: Capstone.

Austin, P. (1976) *How to Do Things with Words*, London: Oxford University Press.

Austin, J., Stevenson, H., and Wei-Skillern, J. (2006) 'Social and Commercial Entrepreneurship: Same, Different, or Both?', in *Entrepreneurship Theory and Practice*, 30(1), pp. 1–22.

Avanzi (2019) Available at: http://www.avanzi.org/en/ (Accessed: 26 Apr. 2019).

Bachmann, M. (2014) 'How the Hub Found Its Centre' [Online]. *Stanford Social Innovation Review*. Available at: http://ssir.org/articles/entry/how_the_hub_found_its_center (Accessed: 10 Jun. 2016).

Bandinelli, C. (2010) *Creative and Social Entrepreneurship: A Critical Analysis*. Unpublished MA dissertation, London: Goldsmiths College.

Bandinelli, C. (2015) *Il Miglior Lavoro del Mondo: Lo Strano Caso dell'Imprenditoria Sociale*, Milano: Doppiozero.

Bandinelli, C. (2019). 'The Production of Subjectivity in Neoliberal Culture Industries: The Case of Coworking Spaces', *International Journal of Cultural Studies*. https://doi.org/10.1177/1367877919878449

Bandinelli, C. and Arvidsson, A. (2013) 'Brand Yourself a Changemaker!', in *Journal of Macromarketing*, 33(1), pp. 67–71.

Bandinelli, C. and Gandini (2019) 'Hubs versus Networks: Towards a Collaborative Individualism' in Gill, R., Pratt, A. and Viriani, T. (eds.) *Creative Hubs in Question: Play Space and Work in the Creative Economy*, London: Palgrave.

Barbrook, R. and Cameron, A. (1995) 'The Californian Ideology' [Online]. *Mute n.3* Available at: https://www.metamute.org/editorial/articles/californian-ideology?source=techstories.org (Accessed: 13 Oct. 2019).

Barinaga, E. (2013) 'Politicising Social Entrepreneurship – Three Social Entrepreneurial Rationalities toward Social Change', in *Journal of Social Entrepreneurship*, 4(3), pp. 347–372.

Bauman, Z. (2006) *Liquid Modernity*, Cambridge: Polity Press.

Bauman, Z. (2000) *The Individualised Society*, Cambridge: Polity Press.

Bauman, Z. (2001) 'Individually Together', preface to Beck, U. and Beck-Gernsheim, E. (eds.) *Individualization: Institutionalized Individualism and Its Social and Political Consequences*, London: SAGE.

Bauwens, M. (2005) 'The Political Economy of Peer Production' [Online]. *CTheory*. Available at: https://journals.uvic.ca/index.php/ctheory/article/view/14464/5306 (Accessed: 13 Oct. 2019).

Beck, U. and Beck-Gernsheim, E. (2001) *Individualization: Institutionalized Individualism and Its Social and Political Consequences*, London: SAGE.

Beck, U., Giddens, A., and Lash, S. (1994) *Reflexive Modernization: Politics, Tradition and Aesthetics in the Modern Social Order*, Cambridge: Polity Press.

Beck, U. and Sznaider, N. (2006) 'Unpacking Cosmopolitanism for the Social Sciences: A Research Agenda', in *British Journal of Sociology*, 57(1), pp. 1–23.

Becker, G. (1994) *Human Capital*, Chicago: University of Chicago Press.

Becker, H. and Geer, B. (1957) 'Participant Observation and Interviewing: A Comparison', in *Human Organization*, 16(3), pp. 28–32.

The Behavioural Design Lab (2013) *Changing Behaviour by Design*. Available at: http://www.designcouncil.org.uk/sites/default/files/asset/document/Changing%20behaviour%20by%20design.pdf (Accessed: 23 Jun. 2016).

Bellanca, N. (2011) 'Elementi di una Teoria dell'Impresa Sociale', AICCON Working Papers 95, Associazione Italiana per la Cultura della Cooperazione e del Non-Profit.

Ben Ner A. e and Gui B. (2003) 'The Theory of Nonprofit Organizations Revisited', in Anheier H. K. e Ben Ner A., *The Study of the Nonprofit Enterprise: Theories and Approaches*, New York: Plenum Publishers.

Benkler, Y. (2006) *The Wealth of Networks: How Social Production Transforms Markets and Freedom*, New Haven, CT: Yale University Press.

Berardi, F. (2001) *La Fabbrica dell'Infelicità: New Economy e Movimento del Cognitariato*, Roma: Map, Derive e Approdi.

Berardi, F. (2009) *The Soul at Work: From Alienation to Autonomy*, Los Angeles: Semiotext(e).

Berardi, F. (2010) *Precarious Rhapsody: Semiocapitalism and the Pathologies of the Post-alpha Generation*, New York: Autonomedia.

Berlinguer, B. (2015) *Servizio Pubblico: Bianca Racconta Enrico Berlinguer*. Available at: http://www.serviziopubblico.it/2015/06/bianca-racconta-enrico-berlinguer/

Bertacchini, E. and Santagata, W. (2012) *Atmosfera creativa*, Bologna: Il Mulino.

Bertilsson, E. (2014) 'The Slippery Relationship between Brand Ethic and Profit', in *Ephemera*, 14(1), pp. 125–136.

Bianchini, F. and Parkinson, M. (1993) *Cultural Policy and Urban Regeneration: The West European Experience*, Manchester: Manchester University Press.

Biehl, J. (2005) *Vita: Life in a Zone of Social Abandonment*, Berkeley: University of California Press.

Bishop, C. (2012) *Artificial Hells: Participatory Arts and the Politics of Spectatorship*, Brooklyn: Verso Books.

Blumer, H. (1998) *Symbolic Interactionism: Perspective and Method*, Berkeley: University of California Press.

Bonini, T. (2013) *Hipster* [Kindle DX e-book], Milano: Doppiozero.

Bonomi, A. (2012) *Milano: le tre città che stanno in una*, Milano: B. Mondadori.

Born. G. (2004) *Uncertain Vision: Birt, Dyke and the Reinvention of the BBC*, London: Secker & Warburg.

Bornstein, D. (2007) *How to Change the World: Social Entrepreneurs and the Power of New Ideas*, Oxford: Oxford University Press.

Bornstein, D. and Davis, S. (2010) *Social Entrepreneurship: What Everyone Needs to Know*, Oxford: Oxford University Press.

Borzaga, C. and Defourny, J. (eds.) (2001) *The Emergence of Social Enterprise*, London: Routledge.

Boschee, J. (2006) *Social Entrepreneurship: The Promises and the Perils*, in Nicholls, A. (eds.) *Social Entrepreneurship New Models of Sustainable Social Change*, Oxford: Oxford University Press.

Botsman, R. and Rogers, R. (2011) *What's Mine Is Yours: How Collaborative Economy Is Changing the Way We Live*, London: Collins.

Bourdieu, P. (1999) *Understanding, in the Weight of the World: Social Suffering in Contemporary Society*, Oxford: Polity.

Boyle, J. (2008). *The Public Domain: Enclosing the Commons of the Mind*, New Haven, CT: Yale University Press.

Brooks, D. (2001) *Bobos in Paradise, the New Upper Class and How They Got There*, New York: Simon & Schuster.

Brouard, F. and Larivet, S. (2010) 'Essay of Clarifications and Definitions of the Related Conceptsof Social Enterprise, Social Entrepreneur and Social Entrepreneurship', in Fayolle, A. and Matlay, H. (eds.) *Handbook of Research on Social Entrepreneurship*, Cheltenham, Northampton: Edward Elgar.

Butler, J. (2002) *What Is Critique? An Essay on Foucault's Virtue*. Available at: https://f.hypotheses.org/wp-content/blogs.dir/744/files/2012/03/butler-2002.pdf (Accessed: 25 Sept. 2016).

Cameron, D. (2013) *Prime Minister: 'Social Investment Can Be a Great Force for Social Change'*. Available at: https://www.gov.uk/government/speeches/prime-ministers-speech-at-the-social-impact-investment-conference (Accessed: 1 Jun. 2016).

Cho, A. (2010) 'Politics, Values and Social Entrepreneurship: A Critical Appraisal', in Mair, J. Robinson, J. and Hockerts, K. (eds.) *Social Entrepreneurship*, Basingstoke: Palgrave Macmillan, pp. 34–57.

Christopherson, S. (2008) 'Beyond the Self-Expressive Creative Worker: An Industry Perspective on Entertainment Media', in *Theory, Culture & Society*, 25, pp. 73–95.

Clark, J. (2007) 'Coworkers of the World Unite' [Online]. *The American Prospect*. Available at: http://prospect.org/article/coworkers-world-unite

Clark, M. (2009) *The Social Entrepreneur Revolution: Doing Good by Making Money, Making Money by Doing Good*, London: Marshall Cavendish Business.

Cleaver, H. (1991) 'Translator Introduction. Part I', in Negri, A. (ed.) *Marx beyond Marx: Lessons on the Grundrisse*, London: Pluto Press.

Clifford, G. (2001) *Available lights: Anthropological Reflections on Philosophical Topics*, Princeton, NJ: Princeton University Press.

Clifford, J. (1992) *Travelling Culture*, in Grossberg, L. Nelson, C. and Treichler P. (eds.) 'Cultural Studies', London: Routledge.

Clifford, J. (1997) *Routes: Travel and Translation in the Late Twentieth Century*, Cambridge, MA: Harvard University Press.

Cohen and Bannick (2014) 'Is Social Impact Investing the Next Venture Capital?' [Online]. *Forbes*. Available at: https://wiki.coworking.org/w/page/35382594/

Coworking%20Manifesto%20%28global%20-%20for%20the%20world%29 (Accessed: 20 Jun. 2016).

Colleoni, E. and Arvidsson, A. (2014) 'Knowledge Sharing and Social Capital Building. The Role of Coworking Spaces in the Knowledge Economy in Milan', Unpublished Report, Office for Youth, Municipality of Milan.

Coworking Manifesto (2016) Available at: https://wiki.coworking.org/w/page/35382594/Coworking%20Manifesto%20%28global%20-%20for%20the%20world%29 (Accessed: 10 Jun. 2016).

Crapanzano, V. (1980) *Tuhami: Portrait of a Moroccan*, Chicago: University of Chicago Press.

Cremin, C. S. (2003) 'Self-Starters, Can-Doers and Mobile Phoneys: Situations Vacant Columns and the Personality Culture in Employment', *The Sociological Review*, 51, pp. 109–128.

Crouch, C. (2011) *The Strange Non-Death of Neo-Liberalism*, Cambridge: Polity.

Cresswell, T. (2006) *On the Move: Mobility in the Modern Western World*, New York: Routledge.

Cresswell, T. (2009) 'Toward a Politics of Mobility. Environment and Planning', in *Society and Space* 28, pp. 17–31.

Davis, S. (2002) *Social Entrepreneurship: Towards an Entrepreneurial Culture of Social and Economic Development* [Online]. Prepared by request for the Youth Employment Summit, Available at: https://papers.ssrn.com/sol3/papers.cfm?abstract_id=978868 (Accessed: 13 Oct. 2019).

Davies, W. (2014) *The Limits of Neoliberalism. Authority, Sovereignty and the Logic of Competition*, London: Polity.

Davies, W. (2015) 'The Return of Social Government: From "Socialist Calculation" to "Social Analytics"', in *European Journal of Social Theory*, April, 15, pp. 1–20.

Dearden-Phillips, C. (2008) *Your Chance to Change the World: The No-Fibbing Guide to Social Entrepreneurship*, London: Directory of Social Change.

Dees, G. J. (1998) *The Meaning of Social Entrepreneurship*. Available at: http://www.caseatduke.org/documents/dees_sedef.pdf (Accessed: Jun. 2016).

Dees, J. G. and Anderson, B. B. (2006) *Framing a Theory of Social Entrepreneurship: Building on Two Schools of Practice and Thought*, in Mosher-Williams, R. (ed.), *Research on Social Entrepreneurship: Understanding and Contributing to an Emerging Field*, 1(3), pp. 39–66.

Deleuze, G. and Guattari, F. (2009) *Anti-Oedipus: Capitalism and Schizophrenia*, New York: Penguin.

Desjarlais, R. (2003) *Sensory Biographies: Lives and Deaths among Nepal's Yolmo Buddhists*, Berkeley: University of California Press.

Defourny, J. and Nyssens, M. (2008) 'Social Enterprise in Europe: Recent Trends and Developments', in *Social Enterprise Journal*, 4(3), pp. 202–228.

Deleuze, G. and Guattari, F. (1987) *A Thousand Plateaux: Capitalism and Schizofrenia*, London: Continuum.

Dey, P. and C. Steyaert (2010) 'The Politics of Narrating Social Entrepreneurship', in *Journal of Enterprising Communities: People and Places in the Global Economy*, 4(1), pp. 85–108.

Dilts, A. (2011) 'From "Entrepreneur of the Self" to "Care of the Self": Neo-Liberal Governmentality and Foucault's Ethics', in *Foucault Studies*, 10(12), pp. 130–146.

Donovan, K. (2011) *Culture and Creativity in the Next Ten Years*, London: DCMS.

Donzelot, J. (1991) *Pleasure in Work*, in Burchell, G. Gordon, C. and Miller, P. (eds.), *The Foucault Effect: Studies in Governmentality*, Chicago: University of Chicago Press.

Donzelot, J. (2008) 'Michel Foucault and Liberal Intelligence', in *Economy and Society*, 37(1), pp. 115–134.

Dowling, E. (2007) 'Producing the Dining Experience: Measure, Subjectivity and the Affective Worker', in *Ephemera*, 7(1), pp. 117–132.

Drayton, B. (2006) 'The Citizen Sector Transformed', in Nicholls, A. (ed.) *Social Entrepreneurship New Models of Sustainable Social Change*, Oxford: Oxford University Press.

Drayton, W. (2007) 'Everyone a Changemaker: Social Entrepreneurship Ultimate Goal' [Online]. *Kosmos Journal of Global Transformation*. Available at: www.kosmosjournal.org/article/everyone-achangemaker-social-entrepreneurship-ultimate-goal/ (Accessed: 08 Jun. 2016).

Drayton, W. (2012) 'Creating an Everyone Is a Changemaker World' [Online]. *Global Education Magazine*. Available at: http://www.globaleducationmagazine.com/creating-changemaker-world/ (Accessed: 20 Jun. 2016).

Drucker, P. (2006) *Innovation and Entrepreneurship: Practice and Principles*, Oxford: Butterworth-Heinemann.

Du Gay, P. (1996) *Consumption and Identity at Work*, London: SAGE.

Dudnik, N. (2010) 'Social Entrepreneurs' Tricky Issues of Sustainability and Scale' [Online]. *Harvard Business Review*. Available at: https://hbr.org/2010/10/social-entrepreneurs-tricky-is (Accessed: 26 Sept. 2016).

Egan-Wyer, C., Louise Muhr, S., Pfeiffer, A. and Svensson, P. (2014) 'The Ethics of the Brand', in *Ephemera* 14(1), pp. 1–11.

Ehrenreich, B. (2009) *Bright-Sided: How the Relentless Promotion of Positive Thinking Has Undermined America*, New York: Metropolitan Books.

Elkington, J. (2008) *The Power of Unreasonable People: How Social Entrepreneurs Create Markets That Change the World*, Boston: Harvard Business.

Faubion, J. D. (2001) 'Toward an Anthropology of Ethics: Foucault and the Pedagogies of Autopoiesis', in *Representations*, 74(1), pp. 83–104.

Faubion, J. D. (2011) *An Anthropology of Ethics*, Cambridge: Cambridge University Press.

Fayolle, A. and Matlay, H. (eds.) (2010) *Handbook of Research on Social Entrepreneurship*, Cheltenham, Northampton: Edward Elgar.

Feyerabend, P. (2010) *Against Method*, London: Verso Books.

Fleming, P. (2009) *Authenticity and the Cultural Politics of Work*, Oxford: Oxford University Press.

Florida, R. (2002) *The Rise of the Creative Class: And How It's Transforming Work, Leisure, Community and Everyday Life*, New York: Basic Books.

Foley, D. E. (1990) *Learning Capitalist Culture: Deep in the Heart of Tejas*, Philadelphia: University of Pennsylvania Press.

Forbes (2016) *30 Under 30 Social Entrepreneurs*. Available at: http://www.forbes.com/30-under-30-2016/social-entrepreneurs/#8d6e41076004 (Accessed: 1 Jun. 2016).

Forkert, K. (2013) *Artistic Lives: A Study of Creativity on Two European Cities*, Farnham, Surrey: Ashgate.

Foucault, M. (1977) 'The Political Function of the Intellectual', in *Radical Philosophy*, 17, pp. 12–14.

Foucault, M. (1991) *Discipline and Punish: The Birth of the Prison*, London: Penguin Books.

Foucault, M. (2000) 'On the Genealogy of Ethics: Overview of Work in Progress', in Rabinow, P. (ed.) *Michel Foucault Ethics, Essential Work of Foucault 1954–1984*, Volume 1, London: Penguin.

Foucault, M. (2005) *The Hermeneutic of the Subject: Lectures at the Collège de France* 1981–1982, Basingstoke: Palgrave Macmillan.

Foucault, M. (2007) *The Politics of Truth*, Los Angeles: Semiotext(e).

Foucault, M. (2010) *The Birth of Biopolitics: Lectures at the Collège de France 1978–1979*, Basingstoke: Palgrave Macmillan.

Foucault, M. (2014) *The Government of the Living: Lectures at the Collège the France 1979–1980*, Basingstoke: Palgrave Macmillan.

Fuchs, M., Fizek, S., Ruffino, P. and Schrape, N. (2014) *Rethinking Gamification*, Lüneburg: Meson Press.

FutureFest (2015) *FutureFest*. Available at: http://www.futurefest.org/2015 (Accessed: 24 Sept. 2016).

FutureFest (2016) *FutureFest*. Available at: http://www.futurefest.org/ (Accessed: 26 Sept. 2016).

Gabriel, M. (2014) *Making It Big: Strategies for Scaling Social Innovation*, London: Nesta.

Gandini, A. (2015) 'The Rise of Coworking Spaces: A Literature Review', in *Ephemera*, 15(1), pp. 193–205.

Gandini, A., Bandinelli, C. and Cossu, A. (2017) '*Competing* Collaborating Coalescing Artists, Freelancers and Social Entrepreneurs as the New Subjects of the Creative Class', In *Collaborative Production in the Creative Industries*, London: University of Westminster Press.

Geertz, C. (1973) *The Interpretation of Cultures: Selected Essays*, New York: Basic Books.

Geertz, C. (1998) 'Deep Hanging Out' [Online]. *The New York Review of Books*, Available at: http://www.nybooks.com/articles/1998/10/22/deep-hanging-out/ (Accessed: 22 Sept. 2016).

GEM (2011) GEM *Report on Social Entrepreneurship, GEM Global Entrepreneurship Monitor*. Available at: http://www.gemconsortium.org/docs/376/gem-report-on-social-entrepreneurship-executive-summary (Accessed: 13 Oct. 2019).

Gill, R. and Pratt, A. (2008) 'In the Social Factory? Immaterial Labour, Precariousness and Cultural Work', in *Theory Culture & Society*, 25(7–8), pp. 1–30.

Gill, R., Pratt. A. and Viriani, T. (eds.) (2019) *Creative Hubs in Question: Play Space and Work in the Creative Economy*, London: Palgrave.

Gillinson, S. Horne, M. and Baeck, P. (2010) *Radical Efficiency*, London: NESTA.

GLA (2015) *London Housing Market Report*. Available at: http://data.london.gov.uk/housingmarket/ (Accessed: 21 Sept. 2016).

Gordon, C. (1987) 'The Soul of the Citizen: Max Weber and Michel Foucault on Rationality and Government', in Whimster S. and Lash S. (eds.) *Max Weber: Rationality and Modernity*, London: Allen and Unwin.

Gordon, M. (2016) *Design Your Life Change the World: Your Path as a Social Entrepreneur*. Available at: http://www.profmichaelgordon.com/book/ (Accessed: 1 Jun. 2016).

GOV.UK (2018) *PM's Social Enterprise Roundtable: 18 June 2018*. Available at: https://www.gov.uk/government/news/pms-social-enterprise-roundtable-18-june-2018 (Accessed: 26 Apr. 2019).

Graeber, D. (2018) *Bullshit Jobs: A Theory*, London: Allen Lane.

Grameen Bank (2016) *Grameen Bank*. Available at: http://www.grameen-info.org/about-us/ (Accessed: 23 Jun. 2016).

Gramsci, A. (1971) *Selections from the Prison Notebooks of Antonio Gramsci*, London: Lawrence and Wishart.

Greif, M. (2010) 'The Hipster in the Mirror' [Online]. *The New York Times*. Available at: http://www.nytimes.com/2010/11/14/books/review/Greif-t.html?_r=0 (Accessed: 26 Sept. 2016).

Gregg, M. (2007) 'Thanks for the Ad(d): Neoliberalism's Compulsory Friendship', talk delivered at the launch of MA in Gender and Culture, London: Goldsmiths University.

Gregg, M. (2011) *Work's Intimacy*, Cambridge: Polity.

Grenier, P. (2003) 'Reclaiming Enterprise for the Social Good: The Political Climate for Social Entrepreneurship in UK', paper presented at the 32nd Annual ARNOVA Conference, Denver, CO.

Grodach, C. and Silver, D. (2013) *The Politics of Urban Cultural Policy: Global Perspectives*, Abingdon: Routledge.

Guardian (2016) *Social Enterprise Blog*. Available at: http://www.theguardian.com/sustainable-business/social-enterprise-blog (Accessed: 29 Jun. 2016).

Gui, B., 1991, 'The Economic Rationale for the Third Sector: Nonprofit and other Noncapitalist Organizations', in *Annals of Public and Cooperative Economics*, 62, pp. 551–572.

Gurnstein, M. (2001) 'Community Informatics, Community Networks and Strategies for Flexible Networking', in Keeble, R. and Loader, D. B. (eds.) *Community Informatics: Shaping Computer-Mediated Social Relations*, London: Routledge.

Hacking, I. (2004) 'Between Michel Foucault and Erving Goffman: Between Discourse in the Abstract and Face to Face Interaction', in *Economy and Society*, 33(3), pp. 277–302.

Hardin, G. (1968) 'The Tragedy of the Commons', in *Science*, 162(3859), pp. 1243–1248.

Hardt, M. and Negri, A. (2009) *Commonwealth*, Cambridge, MA: Belknap Press of Harvard University Press.

Harvey, D. (1989) 'From Managerialism to Entrepreneurialism: The Transformation in Urban Governance in Late Capitalism', in *Geografiska Annaler. Series B, Human Geography*, 71(1), pp. 3–17.

Haugh, H. (2005) 'A Research Agenda for Social Entrepreneurship', in *Social Enterprise Journal*, 1(1), pp. 1–12.

Haugh, H. and Tracey, P. (2004). 'The Role of Social Enterprise in Regional Development', in Cambridge-MIT Institute (ed.) *Social Enterprise and Regional Development Conference, 16 September 2004*, Cambridge-MIT, University of Cambridge, UK. Cambridge: Cambridge-MIT Institute.

Hayek, Friederich A. (2001) *The Road to Serfdom*, London: Routledge.

Hayek, Friederich A. (1996) *Individualism and Economic Order*, Chicago: University of Chicago Press.

Hearn, A. (2008) 'Blowing Up the Brand Meat, Mask, Burden Probing the Contours of the Branded Self', in *Journal of Consumer Culture*, 8(2), pp. 163–183.

Heckscher, C. and Adler, P. (2006) *The Firm as a Collaborative Community*, Oxford: Oxford University Press.

Heidegger, M. (1977) *The Question Concerning Technology and Other Essays*, New York: Harper Perennial.

Heller, M. (1998) 'The Tragedy of the Anticommons: Property in the Transition from Marx to Markets', in *Harvard Law Review*, 111, pp. 621–688.

Heller, M. (2008) *The Gridlock Economy: How Too Much Ownership Wrecks Markets, Stops Innovation, and Costs Lives*, New York: Basic Books.

Hill, T. L., Kohtari, T. H. and Shea, M. (2010) 'Patterns of Meaning in the Social Entrepreneurship Literature: A Research Platform', in *Journal of Social Entrepreneurship*, 1(1), pp. 5–31.

Hjort, D. (2010) 'Ending Essay: Sociality and Economy in Social Entrepreneurship', in Fayolle, A. and Matlay, H. (eds.) *Handbook of Research on Social Entrepreneurship*, Cheltenham, Northampton: Edward Elgar.

Hjort, D. (2013) 'Public Entrepreneurship: Desiring Social Change, Creating Sociality', in *Entrepreneurship and Regional Development: An International Journal*, 25(1–2), pp. 34–51.

Hjorth, D. and Bjerke, B. (2006) 'Public Entrepreneurship: Moving From Social/Consumer to Public/Citizen', in Steyaert, C. and Hjorth D. (eds.), *Entrepreneurship as Social Change*, Cheltenham: Edward Elgar.

Hjorth, D. and Steyaert, C. (2003) 'Entrepreneurship Beyond (a New) Economy: Creative Swarms and Pathological Zones', in Steyaert, C. and Hjorth, D. (eds.) *New Movements in Entrepreneurship*, Cheltenham: Edward Elgar.

Hobsbawn, E. (2002) *Interesting Times: A Twentieth-Century Life*, London: Abacus.

Hursthouse, R. (1999) *On Virtue Ethics*, Oxford: Oxford University Press.

Hyde, L. (2010) *Common as Air: Revolution, Art, and Ownership*, New York: Farrar, Straus and Giroux.

Illouz, E. (2007) *Cold Intimacies*, Cambridge: Polity Press.

Impact Hub (2016) *Impact Hub Network*. Available at: http://www.impacthub.net/ (Accessed: 12 Jun. 2016).

Impact Hub Academy (2016) *Impact Hub Westminster*. Available at http://westminster.impacthub.net/2012/02/29/aenean-et-justo-elit/ (Accessed: 11 Jun. 2016).

Impact Hub Net (2016) *Impact Hub Net*. Available at: http://www.impacthub.net/ (Accessed: 28 Jun. 2016).

Iris Network (2016) *Iris Network*. Available at: http://irisnetwork.it/ (Accessed: 24 Sept. 2016).
Jameson, F. (2003) 'Future City', in *New Left Review*, 21, pp. 65–79.
Kant, I. (1993 [1781]) *Critique of Pure Reason*, London: J. M. Dent; Rutland (Vt.): Charles E. Tuttle.
Kerlin, J. (2006) 'Social Enterprise in the United States and Europe: Understanding and Learning from the Differences', in *Voluntas*, 17(3), pp. 247–263.
Khanin D. (2012) 'Social Entrepreneurship and the Tragedy of the Commons' in Zeyen A., Beckmann, M., Mueller, S., Dees, G., Khanin, D., Krueger, N., Murphy, P. J., Santos, F., Scarlata, M., Walske J. and Zacharakis, A. (eds.) 'Social Entrepreneurship and Broader Theories: Shedding New Light on the "Bigger Picture"', in *Journal of Social Entrepreneurship*, 4(1), pp. 88–103.
Knight, H. F. (2006) *Risk, Uncertainty and Profit*, New York: Dover Publications.
Knox, P. L. (2014) *Atlas of Cities*, Princeton, NJ: Princeton University Press.
Kois, B. (2013) 'Discussing the Social Entrepreneurial Movement as a Means of Provoking Normative Change in West Kalimantan, Indonesia: An Interview with Kinari Webb', in *ASEAS: Austrian Journal of South-East Asian Studies*, 6(1), pp. 188–194.
Kjaerulff, J. (2010) *Internet and Change: An Anthropology of Knowledge and Flexible Work*, Aarhus: Intervention Press.
Kuhn, T. (1996) *The Structure of Scientific Revolution*, Chicago: University of Chicago Press.
Kylin, C. and Karlsson, J. (2008) 'Re-Establishing Boundaries in Home-Based Telework', in Warhurst, C., Eikhof, R. D. and Haunschild, A. *Work Less, Live More?: A Critical Analysis of the Work-Life Boundary*, Basingstoke: Palgrave Macmillan.
Larsen, M., Ferraresi, F., Bandinelli. C., Vitali, M. and Mavroidakos, K. (2012) *HUB Milano Community Mapping*, Milan: Impact Hub.
Laidlaw, J. (2001) 'For an Anthropology of Ethics and Freedom', in *Journal of the Royal Anthropological Institute*, 8, pp. 311–332.
Landry, C. and Bianchini, F. (2005) *The Creative City*, London: DEMOS.
Lange, B. (2006) 'From Cool Britannia to Generation Berlin? Geographies of Culturepreneurs and Their Creative Milieus in Berlin', in Eisenberg, C., Gerlach, R. and Handke, C. (eds.) *Cultural Industries: The British Experience in International Perspective*, Berlin: Humboldt University Berlin.
Lange, B. (2011) 'Re-Scaling Governance in Berlin's Creative Economy', in *Culture Unbound*, 3, pp. 187–208.
Lasch, C. (1991) *The Culture of Narcissism: American Life in an Age of Diminishing Expectations*, London: W. W. Norton & Company.
Lash, S. (2002) *Critique of Information*, London: SAGE.
Lash, S. and Lury, C. (2007) *The Global Culture Industry: The Mediation of Things*, Cambridge: Polity.
Lash, S. and Urry, J. (1987) *The End of Organised Capitalism*, Cambridge: Polity Press.
Latour, B. (2005) *Reassembling the Social*, Oxford: Oxford University Press.
Latour, B. and Wookgar, S. (1986) *The Laboratory Life: The Construction of Scientific Facts*, Princeton, NJ: Princeton University Press.

Lazzarato, M. (1996) 'Immaterial Labour', in Hardt, M. and Virno, P. (eds.) *Radical Thought in Italy: A Potential Politics*, Minneapolis: University of Minnesota Press.

Lazzarato, M. (1997) *Lavoro Immateriale: Forme di vita e produzione di soggettività*, Verona: Ombre Corte.

Lazzarato, M. (2004a) 'From Capital-Labour to Capital-Life', in *Ephemera*, 4(3), pp. 187–208.

Lazzarato, M. (2004b) *La Politica dell'Evento*, Soveria Mannelli: Rubettino.

Lazzarato, M. (2009) 'Neoliberalism in Action: Inequality, Insecurity and the Reconstitution', in *Theory, Culture & Society*, 26, pp. 109–133.

Leadbeater, C. (1997) *The Rise of the Social Entrepreneur*, London: DEMOS.

Lehner, M. and Halliday, S. V. (2014) 'Branding Sustainability', in *Ephemera*, 14(1) pp. 13–34.

Lehner, O. M. and Kansikas, J. (2013) 'Pre-Paradigmatic Status of Social Entrepreneurship Research: A Systematic Literature Review', in *Journal of Social Entrepreneurship*, 4(2), pp. 198–219.

Leslie, D. and Rantisi, N. M. (2011) 'Creativity and Place in the Evolution of a Cultural Industry', in *Urban Studies*, 48(9), pp. 1771–1787.

Levy, N. (2004) 'Foucault as Virtue Ethicist', in *Foucault Studies*, 1, pp. 20–31.

Light, P. C. (2006) 'Reshaping Social Entrepreneurship' [Online]. *Stanford Social Innovation Review*. Available at: https://ssir.org/articles/entry/reshaping_social_entrepreneurship (Accessed: 13 Oct. 2019).

Liu, A. (2004) *The Laws of Cool: Knowledge Work and the Culture of Information*, Chicago: University of Chicago Press.

Lorenzini, D. (2013) 'What Is a Regime of Truth?' [Online]. *Foucault Blog*. Available at: https://michel-foucault.com/2013/10/31/what-is-a-regime-of-truth-2013/ (Accessed: 13 Oct. 2019).

Lorenzini, D. (2016) 'From Counter-Conduct to Critical Attitude: Michel Foucault and the Art of Not Being Governed Quite So Much', in *Foucault Studies*, 21, pp. 7–12.

Lovis, B., Lovis, H. and Howken, P. (1996) 'A Road Map for Natural Capitalism' [Online]. *Harvard Business Review*. Available at: https://hbr.org/2007/07/a-road-map-for-natural-capitalism (Accessed: 26 Sept. 2016).

Lury, C. (2004) *Brands: The Logos of the Global Economy*, London: Routledge.

Lury, C., Parisi, L. and Terranova, T. (2012) 'Introduction: The Becoming Topological of Culture', in *Theory Culture & Society*, 29(3), pp. 3–35.

Lury, C. and Wakeford, N. (eds.) (2012) *Inventive Methods: The Happening of the Social*, London: Routledge.

Lynch, K., Baker, J. and Lyons, M. (2009) *Affective Equality: Who Cares? Studies in Gender, Care and Justice*, London: Palgrave Macmillan.

Marchetti, A., & Gramigna, E. (2007) *Produttori di Stile: Lavoro e Flessibilita nelle Case di Moda Milanesi*, Milano: F. Angeli.

Marcus, G. E. (1995) 'Ethnography in/of the World System: The Emergence of Multi-Sited Ethnography', in *Annual Review of Anthropology*, 24, pp. 95–117.

Martin, L. H., Gotman, H. and Hutton, P. H. (1988) *Technologies of the Self: A Seminar with Michel Foucault*, London: Tavistock.

Marwick, A. (2010) *Status Update: Celebrity Publicity and Self Branding in Web 2.0*, [Online]. PhD. Thesis, New York, New York University. Available at: http://www.tiara.org/blog/wp-content/uploads/2010/09/marwick_dissertation_statusupdate.pdf (Accessed: 25 Sept. 2016).

Marwick, E. A. (2013) *Status Update: Celebrity, Publicity and Self-Branding*, New Haven, CT: Yale University Press.

Maier, F., Schober, C., Simsa, R. and Reihard, M. (2015) 'SROI as a Method for Evaluation Research: Understanding Merits and Limitations', in *Voluntas*, 26(5), pp. 1805–1830.

Mair, J. (2010) 'Social Entrepreneurship: Taking Stock and Looking Ahead', in Fayolle, A. and Matlay, H. (eds.) *Handbook of Research on Social Entrepreneurship*, Cheltenham, Northampton: Edward Elgar.

Mair, J., Robinson, J. and Hockerts, K. (2010) *Social Entrepreneurship*, Basingstoke: Palgrave Macmillan.

Massarsky, C. W. (2006) 'Coming of Age: Social Enterprise Reaches Its Tipping Point. Research on Social Entrepreneurship', ARNOVA occasional paper series, 1(3), 67–88.

Mattei, U. (2011) *The State the Market, and Some Preliminary Question about the Common*. Available at: http://works.bepress.com/ugo_mattei/40 (Accessed: 13 Oct. 2019).

Mawson, A. (2008) *The Social Entrepreneur: Making Communities Work*, London: Atlantic Books.

McAllister, K. E. (2011) *Terrain of Memory: A Japanese Canadian Memorial Project*, Vancouver, BC: University of British Columbia Press.

McCall, G. J. and Simmons, J. L. (eds.) (1969) *Issues in Participant Observation: A Text and Reader*, Reading, MA: Addison-Wesley.

McDermont, Morag (2009) 'Asserting Human Rights Claims: Older People in Residential Care', Unpublished paper presented to workshop on Care and Agency, University of Keele.

McGonigal, J. (2011) *Reality Is Broken: Why Games Make Us Better and How They Can Change the World*, New York: Penguin Press.

McNay, L. (2009) 'Self as Enterprise: Dilemma of Control and Resistance in Foucault's The Birth of Biopolitics', in *Theory Culture & Society*, 26(6), pp. 26–55.

McRobbie, A. (1998) *British Fashion Design: Rag Trade or Image Industry?*, London: Routledge.

McRobbie, A. (2001) 'Everyone Is Creative' [Online]. *Open Democracy*. Available at: http://www.opendemocracy.net/node/652 (Accessed: 13 Oct. 2019).

McRobbie, A. (2002) 'Clubs to Companies: Notes on the Decline of Political Culture in Speeded up Creative Worlds', in *Cultural Studies*, 16(4), pp. 518–531.

McRobbie, A. (2015) *Be Creative: Making a Living in the New Culture Industries*, London: Polity.

McRobbie, A., Strutt, D., Bandinelli, C. and Springer, B. (2016) 'Report CREATe Fashion Micro-Enterprises in London Berlin and Milan. AHRC Funded. Phase 1', Unpublished Research Report for CREATe.

Melucci, A. (1989) *Nomads of the Present: Social Movements and Individual Needs in Contemporary Society*, London: Hutchinson Radius.

Millar, R. and Hall, K. (2012) 'Social Return on Investment (SROI) and Performance Measurement: The Opportunities and Barriers for Social Enterprises in Health and Social Care', in *Public Management Review*, 15(6), pp. 923–941.

Molé, N. J. (2010) 'Precarious Subjects: Anticipating Neoliberalism in Northern Italy's Workplaces', *in American Anthropologist*, 112(1), pp. 38–53.

Moriset, B. (2014) 'Building New Places of the Creative Economy. The Rise of Coworking Spaces', Proceedings of the 2nd Geography of Innovation, International Conference 2014, Utrecht University, Utrecht (The Netherlands).

Morozov, E. (2013) *To Save Everything Click Here: The Folly of Technological Solutionism* [Kindle DX e-book], New York: Public Affairs.

Mouffe, C. (2005) *On the Political*. London: Routledge.

Mulgan, G. (2006) 'Cultivating the Other Invisible Hand of Social Entrepreneurship: Comparative Advantage, Public Policy, and Future Research Priorities', in Nicholls, A. (ed.) *Social Entrepreneurship, New Models of Sustainable Social Change*, Oxford: Oxford University Press.

Narayan, K. (2003) [1997] 'How Native Is a "Native" Anthropologist?', in Lewis, R. and Mills, S. (eds.) *Feminist Postcolonial Theory: A Reader*, Edinburgh: Edinburgh University Press.

Negri, A. (1991) *Marx beyond Marx: Lessons on the Grundrisse*, London: Pluto Press.

Negri, A. (2008) *The Porcelain Workshop: For a New Grammar of Politics*, Los Angeles: Semiotext(e).

Negri, A. and Hardt, M. (1999) 'Value and Affect', in *Boundary 2*, 26(2), pp. 77–88.

Negri, A. and Hardt, M. (2003) *Labour of Dyonysus: A Critique of the State-Form*, Minneapolis: University of Minnesota Press.

Nesta (2006) *Nesta Annual Report 2005/2006 Transforming UK Innovation*, London: NESTA.

Nesta (2016) *Our History*. Available at: http://www.nesta.org.uk/about-us/our-history (Accessed: 1 Jun. 2016).

Nicholls, A. (2006) *Social Entrepreneurship, New Models of Sustainable Social Change*, Oxford: Oxford University Press.

Nicholls, A. (2010) 'Editorial: Continuations and Beginnings', in *Journal of Social Entrepreneurship*, 1(1), pp. 1–4.

Nicholls, A. (2013) 'Editorial: Heroes', in *Journal of Social Entrepreneurship*, 4(2), pp. 109–112.

Nicholls, J., Lawlor, E., Neitzert, E. and Goodspeed, T. (2009) *A Guide to Social Return on Investment*, London: Office of the Third Sector, The Cabinet Office.

Niessen, B. (2007) 'Città Creative: Una Rassegna Critica sulla Letteratura e Sulle Definizioni', working paper UrbEur PhD, 10/2007 University of Milano-Bicocca.

Niessen, B. (2009) 'Going Commercial: L'integrazione degli Artisti Underground a Milano e Berlino', working paper UrbEur PhD 07/2009 University of Milano-Bicocca.

Niessen, B. and Zanoni, D. (2016) *CheFare: Analisi e Prospettive tra Impresa Sociale ed Innovazione Culturale*. Available at: http://irisnetwork.it/wp-content/uploads/2015/04/2013-niessen-zanoni.pdf (Accessed: 23 Sept. 2016).

Nyssens, M. (ed.) (2006) *Social Enterprise: At the Crossroad of Market, Public Policies and Civic Society*, New York: Routledge.

Nyssens, M. and Defourny, J. (2010) 'Conceptions of Social Enterprise and Social Entrepreneurship in Europe and the United States: Convergences and Divergences', in *Journal of Social Entrepreneurship*, 1(1), pp. 32–53.

Oakley, A. (1981) 'Interviewing Women: A Contradiction in Terms', in Roberts, H. (ed.) *Doing Feminist Research*, London: Routledge & Kegan Paul.

Obama, B. (2015) *Remarks by the President at Global Entrepreneurship Event*. Available at: https://www.whitehouse.gov/the-press-office/2015/05/11/remarks-president-global-entrepreneurship-event (Accessed: 1 Jun. 2016).

Obi-One (2009) *Primo Rapport Nazionale sull'Altra Economia in Italia*. Available at: http://base.socioeco.org/docs/rapporto_ae_definitivo_15settembre2009.pdf (Accessed: 13 Oct. 2019).

Osterwalder, A. and Pigneur, Y. (2010) *Business Model Generation: A Handbook for Visionaries, Game Changers, and Challengers*, Hoboken, NJ: Wiley.

Ostrom, E. (1990) *Governing the Commons: The Evolution of Institutions for Collective Action. The Political Economy of Institutions and Decisions*, Cambridge: Cambridge University Press.

d'Ovidio, M. (2015) 'The Field of Fashion Production in Milan: a Theoretical Discussion and an Empirical investigation', in *City, Culture and Society*, 6(2), pp. 1–8.

d'Ovidio, M. (2016) *The Creative City Does Not Exist. Critical Essays on the Creative and Cultural Economy of Cities*, Milano: Ledizioni.

d'Ovidio, M., and Pradel, M. (2013) 'Social Innovation and Institutionalisation in the Cognitive-Cultural Economy: Two Contrasting Experiences from Southern Europe', in *Cities*, 33, pp. 69–76.

Oxford Dictionaries (2016a) *Hipster*. Available at: https://en.oxforddictionaries.com/definition/hipster (Accessed: 26 Sept. 2016).

Oxford Dictionaries (2016b) *Platform*. Available at: https://en.oxforddictionaries.com/definition/platform (Accessed: 26 Sept. 2016).

Oxford Hub (2016) *Oxford Hub*. Available at: https://www.oxfordhub.org/ (Accessed: 24 Sept. 2016).

Pandian, A. (2010) 'Interior Horizons: An Ethical Space of Selfhood in South India', in *Journal of the Royal Anthropological Institute* (N.S.), 16, pp. 64–83.

Patel, N. (2015) '90% of Start-Ups Fail: Here's What You Need to Know about the 10%' [Online]. *Forbes*. Available at: https://www.forbes.com/sites/neilpatel/2015/01/16/90-of-startups-will-fail-heres-what-you-need-to-know-about-the-10/#7c1833df6679 (Accessed: 1 May 2019).

Peck, J. (2005) 'Struggling with the Creative Class', in *International Journal of Urban and Regional Research*, 29(4), pp. 740–770.

Peredo, A. M. (2005) 'Community Venture, in "Agua Dulce"', in *Journal of Applied Behavioral Science*, 41(4), pp. 458–481.

Perkone, L. (2012) *The Hub: Success Stories*. Available at: https://www.youtube.com/watch?v=dZ0S2BtWocs (Accessed: 25 Sept. 2016).

Perulli, P. (2015) Un'agenda per Milano Globale. Imprese&Città e Rivista Della Camera Di Commercio Di Milano, 6.

Peters, T. (1997) 'The Brand Called You' [Online]. *Fast Company*. Available at: http://www.fastcompany.com/28905/brand-called-you (Accessed: 13 Oct. 2019).

Pianta, M. (2009) 'L'Altra Economia tra Mercato e Società Civile', in *Sociologia del Lavoro*, 113, pp. 49–66.

Pratt, A. (2011) 'The Cultural Contradictions of the Creative City', in *City, Culture and Society*, 2(3), pp. 123–130.

Pruijt, H. (2004) 'Squatters in the Creative City: Rejoinder to Justus Uitermark', in *International Journal of Urban and Regional Research*, 28(3), pp. 699–705.

Pruijt, H. (2013) 'The Logic of Urban Squatting', in *International Journal of Urban and Regional Research*, 37(1), pp. 19–45.

Rabinow, P. (2000) 'Introduction', in Rabinow, P. (ed.) *Michel Foucault Ethics: Essential Work of Foucault 1954–1984*, Volume One, London: Penguin.

Rancière, J. (2006) *Hatred of Democracy*, London: Verso.

Rawls, J. (1993) *Political Liberalism*, New York: Columbia University Press.

RENA (2016) *RENA Progetto Festival delle Comunità del Cambiamento*. Available at: http://www.progetto-rena.it/festival-2015/ (Accessed: 24 Sept. 2016).

Ricoeur, P. (1994) *Oneself as Another*, Chicago: University of Chicago Press.

Ridley-Duff, R. and Bull, M. (2011) *Understanding Social Enterprise: Theory and Practice*, London: SAGE.

Rosaldo, R. (1989) *Culture and Truth: The Remaking of Social Analysis*, Boston: Beacon Press.

Rose, N. (1989) 'Governing the Enterprising Self', Paper presented at a Conference on the Values of the Enterprise Culture, University of Lancaster, September. Also published in P. Heelas and P. Morris (eds.), *The Values of the Enterprise Culture: the Moral Debate*, London: Routledge.

Rose, N. (1990) *Governing the Soul: the Shaping of the Private Self*, London: Routledge.

Ross, A. (2004) *No-Collar: The Humane Workplace and Its Hidden Costs*, Philadelphia: Temple University Press.

Ross, A. (2008) 'The New Geography of Work: Power to the Precarious?', in *Theory Culture & Society*, 25(7–8), pp. 31–49.

Rouse, R. (1991) 'Mexican Migration and the Social Space of Postmodernity, in *Diaspora*, 1(1), pp. 8–23.

Salamon, L. M., Sokolowski, S. W. and associates (2004) *Global Civil Society: Dimensions of the Nonprofit Sector*, Vol. 2, Bloomfield, CT: Kumarian Press.

Santos, F. (2012) 'A Positive Theory of Social Entrepreneurship', in *Journal of Business Ethics,* 111(3), pp. 335–351.

Sassen, S. (2001) *The Global City: New York, London, Tokyo*, Princeton, NJ: Princeton University Press.

Sassen, S. (2005) 'The Global City: Introducing a Concept', in *The Brown Journal of World Affairs*, XX(2), pp. 27–43.

Say, J. B. (2005) [1832] A Treatise on Political Economy: Or the Production Distribution and Consumption of Wealth, Scholarly Publishing Office, University of Michigan Library.

Schumper, J. A. (1942) *Capitalism, Socialism and Democracy*, London: Allen & Unwin.

Schumpeter, J. A. (1989 [1934]) *The Theory of Economic Development*, Cambridge, MA: Harvard University Press.

Schumpeter, J. A. (1989 [1937]). *Preface to the Japanese edition of Theorie der Wirtschaftlichen Entwicklung*, in R. V. Clemence (ed.), *Essays on Entrepreneurs, Innovations, Business Cycles and the Evolution of Capitalism* (pp. 165–168), New Brunswick, NJ: Transaction Publishers.

Scofield, M. R. (2011) *The Social Entrepreneur's Handbook: How to Start, Build and Run a Business That Improves the World*, New York: McGraw-Hill.

Scott, A. J. (2006) 'Creative Cities: Conceptual Issues and Policy Questions', in *Journal of Urban Affairs*, 28(1), pp. 1–17.

Seale, Clive (ed.) (2004) *Researching Society and Culture*, London: SAGE.

Seanor, P., Bull, M. and Baines, S. (2011) 'Context, Narratives, Drawings and Boundary Objects: Where Social Enterprises Draw the Line' [Online]. Institute of Small Business and Entrepreneurship Conference, University of Sheffield, 9–10 November available at: https://uwe-repository.worktribe.com/output/958177/context-narratives-drawings-boundary-objects-where-social-enterprises-draw-the-line (Accessed: 13 Oct. 2019).

Sen, A. K. (1986) 'Adam Smith's Prudence'. In Lall, S. and Stewart, F. (eds.) *Theory and Reality in Development*, London: Macmillan.

Sennett. R. (1998) *The Corrosion of Character: The Personal Consequences of Work in the New Capitalism*, New York: W. W. Norton.

Sennett, R. (2009) *The Craftman*, London: Penguin.

Sharir, M. and Lerner, M. (2006) 'Gauging the Success of Social Ventures Initiated by Individual Social Entrepreneurs', in *Journal of World Business*, 41(1), pp. 6–20.

Skeggs, B. (1995) *Theorising, Ethics and Representation, in Feminist Ethnography, in Feminist Cultural Theory: Process and Production*, edited by Beverley Skeggs, Manchester: Manchester University Press.

Skoll Centre for Social Entrepreneurship (2016) *Skoll*. Available at: http://www.sbs.ox.ac.uk/faculty-research/skoll (Accessed: 1 Jun. 2016).

Skoll Foundation (2016) *About Jeff Skoll*. Available at: http://skoll.org/about/about-skoll/ (Accessed: 1 Jun. 2016).

Smith, A. (1991 [1776]) *The Wealth of Nations*, London: Everyman's Library.

Smith, A. (2006) *The Theory of the Moral Sentiments*, New York: Dover Publications.

Smith, H. E. (2000) 'Semicommon Property Rights and Scattering in the Open Fields', in *Journal of Legal Studies*, 29, pp. 131–169.

Smith, W. K., Gonin, M. and Besharov, M. L. (2013) 'Managing Social-Business Tensions: A Review and Research Agenda for Social Enterprise', in *Business Ethics Quarterly*, 23(3), pp. 407–442.

Social Enterprise UK (2016) *About Social Enterprise UK*. Available at: http://www.socialenterprise.org.uk/about/about-us (Accessed: 1 Jun. 2016).

Social Impact International (2016) *About Social Impact International*. Available at: http://social-impact.org/about-social-impact-international (Accessed: 24 Sept. 2016).

Sopranizetti, C. (2013) *The Owners of the Map: Motorcycle Taxi Drivers, Mobility and Politics in Bangkok*. Available at: http://nrs.harvard.edu/urn-3:HUL.InstRepos:11169780 (Accessed: Jun. 2016).

Spear, R. (2011) Working Paper Innovation and Collective Entrepreneurship. Chantier de l'économie sociale. https://www.researchgate.net/publication/277036127_Working_Paper_Innovation_and_Collective_Entrepreneurship/citation/download (Accessed: 13 Oct. 2019).

Spinuzzi, C. (2012) 'Working Alone Together. Coworking as Emergent Collaborative Activity', in *Journal of Business and Technical Communication*, 26(4), pp. 399–441.

Spreitzer, G., Bacevice, P. and Garrett, L. (2015) 'Why People Thrive in Coworking Spaces' [Online]. *Harvard Business Review*. Available at: https://hbr.org/2015/05/why-people-thrive-in-coworking-spaces (Accessed: 10 Jun. 2016).

Sprinkler, G. K. (2005) *Beyond Fundraising: New Strategies for Nonprofit Innovation and Investment*, Hoboken, NJ: John Wiley and Sons.

Stark, D. (2009) *The Sense of Dissonance: Accounts of Worth in Economic Life*, Princeton, NJ: Princeton University Press.

Steyaert, C. and Hjort, D. (eds.) (2006) *Entrepreneurship as Social Change*, Cheltenham, UK: Edward Elgar.

Stiegler, B. (2010) *For a New Critique of Political Economy*, Cambridge: Polity Press.

Swyngedouw, E. (2010) 'Apocalypse Forever? Post-Political Populism and the Spectre of Climate Change', in *Theory, Culture & Society*, 27(2–3), pp. 213–232.

Terranova, T. (2000) 'Labor: Producing Culture for the Digital Economy', in *Social Text*, 63(2), pp. 33–58.

Think Public (2016) *Think Public*. Available at: http://thinkpublic.com/ (Accessed: 20 Jun. 2016).

Thrift, N. (1998) 'Virtual Capitalism: The Globalisation of Reflexive Business Knowledge', in Carrier, G. J. and Miller, D. (eds.) *Virtualism: A New Political Economy*, Oxford: Berg.

Thrift, N. (2005) *Knowing Capitalism*, London: SAGE.

Thompson, J. (2002) 'The World of the Social Entrepreneur', in *The International Journal of Public Sector Management*, 15(4–5), pp. 412–431.

Toscano, A. (2003) *Antagonism and Insurrection in Italian Operaismo*. Unpublished article. Available at: http://www.gold.ac.uk/csisp/works/byauthor/t/#d.en.8780 (Accessed: 25 Sept. 2016).

Unltd (2015) *New Research Shows British Entrepreneurs Appetite to Run Business with Social Purpose*. Available at: https://unltd.org.uk/2015/09/04/new-research-shows-british-entrepreneurs-appetite-run-businesses-social-purpose/ (Accessed: 23 Jun. 2016).

Unltd (2016a) *Social Entrepreneurship Award Toolkit*. Available at: http://unltd.org.uk/wp-content/uploads/2012/12/full-toolkit1.pdf (Accessed: 20 Jun. 2016).

Unltd (2016b) *Unltd*. Available at: https://unltd.org.uk/ (Accessed: 24 Sept. 2016).

Urry, J. (2007) *Mobilities*, Cambridge: Polity.

Virno, P. (2003) *A Grammar of the Multitude*, Los Angeles: Semiotext(e).

Vivant, E. (2009) 'How Underground Culture Is Changing Paris', in *Urban Research & Practice*, 2(1), pp. 36–52.

Waltz, M., Hingston, S. and Andéhn, M. (2014) 'The Magic of Ethical Brands', in *Ephemera*, 14(1), pp. 57–80.

Warshaw, S. and Kreamer, A. (2012) The Rise of Coworking Spaces [Online]. *Harvard Business Review*. Available at: https://hbr.org/2012/09/the-rise-of-coworking-office (Accessed: 12 Jun. 2016).

Weber, M. (2009) *From Max Weber. Essays in Sociology*, Oxon: Routledge.

Weber, M. (2014) *The Protestant Ethic and the Spirit of Capitalism*, London: Routledge.

Wegner-Trayner, E. and Wegner-Trayner, B. (2015) *Communities of Practice: A Brief Introduction*. Available at: http://wenger-trayner.com/wp-content/uploads/2015/04/07-Brief-introduction-to-communities-of-practice.pdf (Accessed: 26 Sept. 2016).

Williams, D. K. (2013) *The 4 Essential Traits of Intrapreneurs*. Available at: URL=http://www.forbes.com/sites/davidkwilliams/2013/10/30/the-4-essential-traits-of-intrapreneurs/&refURL=&referrer=#! (Accessed: 24 Sept. 2016).

Willis, P. (1981) *Learning to Labour: How Working Class Kids Get Working Class Jobs*, New York: Columbia University Press.

Wilson, J. and Swyngedouw, E. (eds.) (2014) *The Post-Political and Its Discontents: Spaces of Depoliticisation, Spectres of Radical Politics*, Edinburgh: Edinburgh University Press.

Wittel, A. (2001) 'Toward a Network Sociality', in *Theory Culture & Society*, 18(6), pp. 51–76.

Wolf, D. L. (Ed.) (1996) *Feminist Dilemmas in Fieldwork*, Boulder, CO: Westview.

Wright Mills, C. (1951) *White Collar: The American Middle Classes*, Oxford: Oxford University Press.

Young, R. (2006) 'For What It Is Worth: Social Value and the Future of Social Entrepreneurship', in Nicholls (ed.) *Social Entrepreneurship New Models for Sustainable Social Change*, Oxford: Oxford University Press.

Zappala, G. and Lyons, M. (2009) 'Recent Approaches to Measuring Social Impact on the Third Sector: An Overview', in *Background Paper No. 5*, Centre for Social Impact, University of New South Wales.

Zeyen A., Beckmann, M., Mueller, S., Dees, G., Khanin, D., Krueger, N., Murphy, P.J., Santos, F., Scarlata, M., Walske J. and Zacharakis, A. (2012) 'Social Entrepreneurship and Broader Theories: Shedding New Light on the "Bigger Picture"', in *Journal of Social Entrepreneurship*, 4(1), pp. 88–107.

Žižek, S. (1999) *The Ticklish Subject – The Absent Centre of Political Ontology*, London: Verso Books.

Index

About the Authors

Carolina Bandinelli is Assistant Professor in Media and Creative Industries at the University of Warwick.

www.ingramcontent.com/pod-product-compliance
Ingram Content Group UK Ltd.
Pitfield, Milton Keynes, MK11 3LW, UK
UKHW012042150926
475560UK00001B/148

9 781786 611079